SAVARIC DE MAULÉON

*

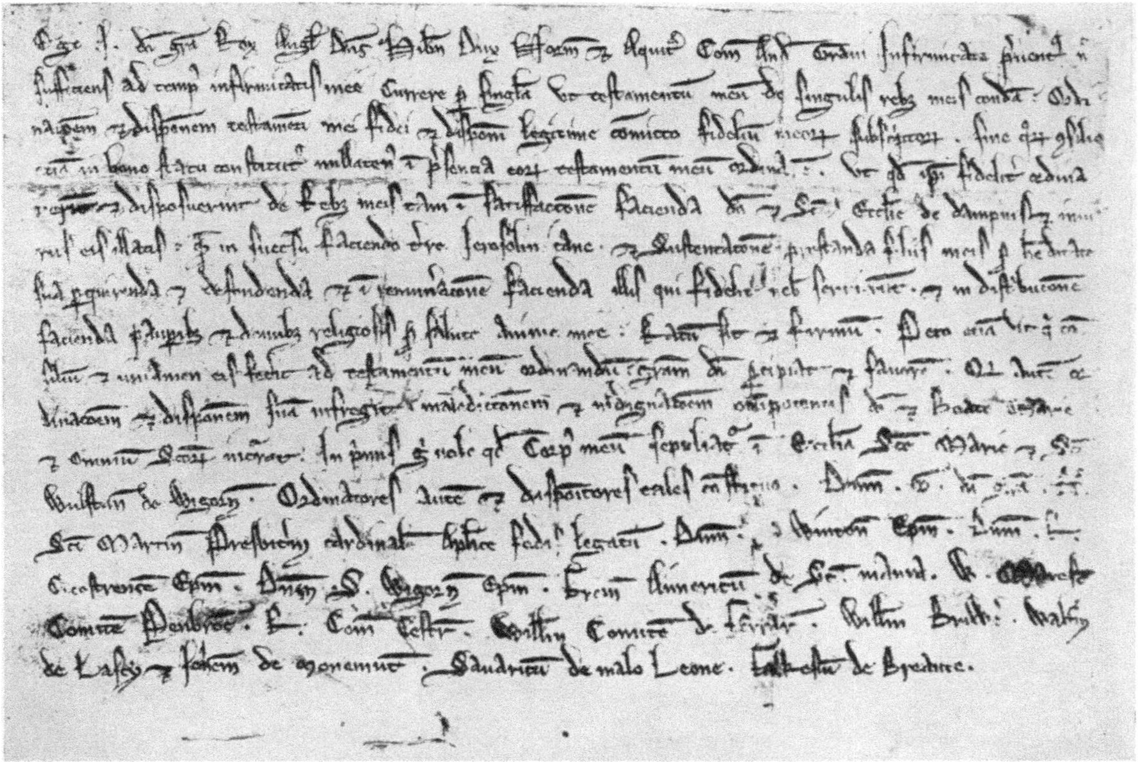

King John's Will

SAVARIC DE MAULÉON

Baron and Troubadour

*

H. J. CHAYTOR, Litt.D.
Master of St Catharine's College
Cambridge

CAMBRIDGE
AT THE UNIVERSITY PRESS
1939

CAMBRIDGE
UNIVERSITY PRESS

University Printing House, Cambridge CB2 8BS, United Kingdom

Cambridge University Press is part of the University of Cambridge.

It furthers the University's mission by disseminating knowledge in the pursuit of
education, learning and research at the highest international levels of excellence.

www.cambridge.org
Information on this title: www.cambridge.org/9781107585560

© Cambridge University Press 1939

First published 1939
First paperback edition 2015

A catalogue record for this publication is available from the British Library

ISBN 978-1-107-58556-0 Paperback

CONTENTS

*

Preface		*page* ix
Bibliography		xi
Chapter I	The Baron	1
Chapter II	The Troubadour	63
Appendices		81
Index		95

ILLUSTRATIONS

*

PLATES

King John's Will   *frontispiece*

Corfe Castle to-day   *facing page* 14

Corfe Castle in 1643   35

IN THE TEXT

Savaric de Mauléon's seal (obverse)   *Title page*

Savaric de Mauléon's coinage   *page* 60

Savaric de Mauléon's seal (reverse)   79

PREFACE

*

SAVARIC DE MAULÉON has an interest for
English readers as being the only troubadour of
whose residence in this country we have definite
evidence from contemporary records. Bernard de
Ventadorn came over in the train of Henry II, but the
evidence for this visit, which there is no reason to doubt,
rests upon the statements of his own poems. The visit of
Marcabru is legendary. While Savaric has his place in
every history of Provençal literature, no one has so far
attempted a detailed history of his life; "dels sieus bons
faich se poiria far un gran libre, qui lo volgues escrire",
"of his exploits there might be made a great book, if
anyone would write it", says his biographer. Such a
book wanders far from the fields of literature, but it can
provide a portrait of the continental baron who travelled
between France and England, fought, intrigued, plundered, governed, and when occasion allowed, maintained a court at which poetry and song were encouraged
and patronised. Such men, for there were doubtless
others of the kind whose less distinguished names have
perished, were not without influence upon the literature
of this country, as I have attempted to show elsewhere.

The fullest account of Savaric that has appeared in
France is the study by B. Ledain, "Savary de Mauléon
et le Poitou à son époque", which deserved a better
fate than interment in the somewhat obscure pages of

La Revue poitevine et saintongeaise of the year 1892. The author has made good use of local records, some of which are not accessible to readers in this country; I have to acknowledge my obligations to his researches in this respect. But he passes very summarily over Savaric's English connections; there are some two hundred references to Savaric in our Close, Patent, and Charter Rolls, not to speak of those in chronicles more or less contemporary; of these sources little use has been made by Ledain or by others mentioned in the bibliography. I have to thank Sir Ivor Atkins, Librarian of the Chapter Library at Worcester Cathedral, for the copy of King John's will with Savaric's attestation.

H. J. C.

November, 1938

BIBLIOGRAPHY

*

ARCÈRE, LOUIS ÉTIENNE. *Histoire de la Ville de La Rochelle.* 1756.

ATGIER, M. *Les Sires de Mauléon, seigneurs de l'île de Ré,* 1137–1268. (Extrait des mémoires de l'Académie des sciences et belles-lettres d'Angers.) Angers, 1898.

BOUQUET, DOM MARTIN. *Rerum Gallicarum et Francicarum Scriptores.* Paris, 1738–1840.

DE LA FONTENELLE. "Savari de Mauléon", *Revue Anglo-française,* 2me série, II, pp. 309 ff.

DE MAZIÈRES (-MAULÉON), LE VICOMTE, "Savary de Mauléon", *La Revue Héraldique,* Paris, 1905, XXI, pp. 273–90.

DUPONT, M. *Histoire de la Rochelle.* La Rochelle, 1830.

GUERINIÈRE, J. *Histoire du Poitou.* Poitiers, 1838.

LEDAIN, B. "Savary de Mauléon et le Poitou à son époque", *La Revue poitevine et saintongeaise,* 1892.

MEYER, P. "La Prise de Damiette, relation inédite en provençal", *Bibliothèque de l'École des Chartes,* XXXVIII (année 1877), pp. 497 ff.

—— *L'Histoire de Guillaume le Maréchal.* 3 vols. Paris, 1891.

MICHEL, FRANCISQUE, éd. *Histoire des Ducs de Normandie et des Rois d'Angleterre.* (Société de l'Histoire de France.) Paris, 1840.

NORGATE, KATE. *John Lackland.* London, 1902.

—— *The Minority of Henry III.* London, 1912.

PETIT-DUTAILLIS, CH. "Étude sur la vie et le règne de Louis VIII", *Bibliothèque de l'École des Hautes Études,* Paris, 1894, fasc. CI.

RAMSAY, J. H. *The Angevin Empire.* London, 1903. (In the list of authorities at the end of this work will be found an account of writers briefly mentioned in the footnotes to this book.)

RICHARD, A. *Histoire des Comtes de Poitou,* 778–1204. 2 vols. Paris, 1903.

THIBAUDEAU, A. R. H. *Histoire du Poitou.* Niort, 1839.

I
THE BARON

*

MAULÉON is now the little town of Châtillon-sur-Sèvre, about half way between Nantes and Poitiers. In 1736 the name was changed to provide a titular seat for a certain Count of Châtillon. Some ruins are still to be seen of a castle standing upon a promontory which descends steeply to the river L'Oing; a vaulted gateway and two towers alone remain of Savaric's family fortress. That family[1] first appears in records about the year 1090; a Raoul de Mauléon is mentioned in charters of donation about 1085 and in 1094 and 1099. A Foulques de Mauléon is also mentioned in a document of this period, but his relationship to Raoul cannot be traced. Raoul had three sons, Savaric I, Raoul II and Ebles. Savaric left two sons, Savaric II and Aimeric, but upon his death the property went to Raoul II by the *droit de viage* or *droit de retour*, which was in force in this family as in other Poitevin families, such as the Viscounts of Thouars and the Sieurs of Parthenay-Larchévêque. Under this custom real property was inherited by all children in turn and in order of age. Thus, on the death of the holder of a fief, his sons inherited only his personal property; the fief went to their eldest uncle, and his eldest nephew did not inherit until all his uncles were dead. But the uncle in possession enjoyed only the usufruct; he could not alienate any part of the fief without the consent of his eldest nephew, the eventual heir. This custom, which was not abolished until 1514, was no doubt intended to modify the hardships caused by the right of primogeni-

[1] See Appendix 1.

ture; it may have been the cause of the occasional family dissensions with which we meet at a later date. Raoul II died before 1155 and his brother Ebles came into the property; he was already Lord of Talmond by his marriage with Eustachie de Lezay, who died in 1170; he also became Lord of La Rochelle. He left two children, Raoul III and Guillaume, and as the other branch had died out, Raoul III succeeded to the considerable estates about 1180. He is mentioned by the troubadour Bertran de Born in his *sirventes* "Puois Ventadorns" (Appel, no. 11, p. 28): this was a manifesto of the league formed against Richard Cœur de Lion in the early part of 1183, as a result of Richard's quarrels with his elder brother, the "Young King"; Bertran hoped that Raoul would join his side. Raoul accompanied Richard on his crusade in 1190[1] and was rescued by the king from capture by the Saracens at the battle of Joppa. He married one Alix de Ré and died about 1202,[2] leaving three children, Savaric III, Eustachie, Viscountess of Chatellerault, and Jeanne, Viscountess of Rochechouart. Raoul's possessions had been recognised by Henry II in a document, undated but belonging apparently to the middle years of his reign: "Rex confirmavit Radulpho de Maleon et Willielmo de Maleon et Savarico filio ejusdem Radolphi totum Talemondeis et les Mostiers des Mafels et Curson cum omnibus pertinentibus de Talemondeis...ac etiam rex concessit praefato Radulpho et Willielmo et Savarico decem milia solidorum monetae annuatim percipienda in praeposi-

---

[1] *Gallia Christiana*, II, p. 1403.

[2] Savaric signed no document before this date, which is also the date of the first mention of him in P. Meyer, *L'Histoire de Guillaume le Maréchal*, l. 12158. (R. Lejeune, *L'œuvre de Jean Renart*, Liège, 1935, p. 100.)

tum de Rupella."[1] William was the younger brother of Raoul and the uncle of Savaric; all three are mentioned in this document as heirs under the *droit de viage*.

The date of Savaric's birth cannot be stated with any certainty; it was before 1180, as his name appears in a charter of that date. The troubadour biography speaks of him as a "rics baros" of Poitou, that is, as the lord of extensive possessions; he may have obtained these or some of them before the death of his uncle by John's donation in 1204 (see p. 15). His uncle died in 1214. The biography gives a list of his possessions which are identified by Chabaneau as follows: Talmont, in La Vendée (arrondissement des Sables-d'Olonne), Fontenay-le-Comte (La Vendée), Châtelaillon (Charente Inférieure), Bouhet (Charente Inférieure, arrondissement de Rochefort, canton d'Aigrefeuille), Benon (arrondissement de la Rochelle, canton de Courçon), Saint-Michel-en-l'Erm (arrondissement de Fontenay-le-Comte), l'île de Ré, Angoulins (arrondissement de la Rochelle) and two places, the islands of Nives and of Nestrine, identification of which is doubtful. He married Belle-Assez, daughter of Guillaume de Chantemerle, Lord of Pouzauges and Pareds, an inheritance perhaps included in the "many other fair places" accorded to him by his biographer, who praises him highly: "A fair knight was he, courteous and instructed, and generous above all generous men. More than anyone in the world he liked gifts and ladies' service and tourneys and song and amusement and composing poems, holding courts and

---

[1] MS. Harl. 311, f. 130 r. (S. d'Ewesii collectanea plerumque historica); *Romania*, L, January 1924, p. 98. This was continued by John in 1199 with modifications of rights over La Rochelle: see Appendix 2.

showing generosity. More than any other knight he was the true friend of ladies and lovers, and was anxious to meet good men and to do them pleasure. And he was the best warrior that ever was in the world. Sometimes he was fortunate and at times came to harm. And all the wars which he had were with the King of France and his men." This statement is entirely incorrect, as are very many statements in these biographies. "And of his exploits there might be made a great book, if anyone would write it, of one who was most modest, merciful and true, and did more fine deeds than any man whom I ever saw or heard of, and was minded to do yet more." Savaric's life covers a period within which the feudal nationalities were broken up and the unification of France was begun. The Albigeois crusade and the collapse of the Anglo-Norman rule were the two events which chiefly contributed to further this process of change. No violent efforts were at first required of the French crown. Philippe Auguste and Louis were able to utilise other forces for their own ends: the religious fanaticism of de Montfort's crusaders and the incompetence of John gave them a foothold which the Hundred Years' Wars and the battles of Crécy, Agincourt and Poitiers could not permanently endanger. Provençal gave way to French, the troubadour was forced to emigrate, the society which had supported him decayed, feudal independence was broken down and the brother of the King of France became Count of Poitou.

The Poitevin nobles gained a reputation for inconsistency and unreliability;[1] they shifted their allegiance

---

[1] See Meyer, *Le Maréchal*, III, p. 24 n. 3, where allusions to this subject are collected.

from one overlord to another upon no discoverable principle or pledge except their own self-interest. It must be said for them that it cannot have been always easy to decide where their obligations lay. The fact that the county of Poitou was united with the duchy of Aquitaine was a cause of various complications. Richard Cœur de Lion had been made both duke and count in 1176 or 1179: whether this appointment abrogated the rights of his mother Eleanor is not clear: in 1185 he was obliged to return Poitou and probably also the duchy to Eleanor, and her rights, in any case, reverted to her at the end of his reign. Richard had given the county of Poitou to his nephew, Otho of Saxony, whose tenure lapsed when he was chosen King of Germany in 1198, in the year before Richard's death. The title of Duke of Aquitaine, though conjoined with that of Count of Poitou, was, in fact, purely conventional and nothing more than part of the formula that appeared in the protocols of acts and deeds. Geographically speaking, the northern part of Aquitaine was Poitou; the southern part, from Bordeaux and including the archdiocese of Auch, was Gascony. These two provinces had separate seneschals and administrations. When Otho assumed the title, Gascony was not his to govern; it was part of the dowry of Berengaria, Richard's queen, and there is no evidence that Richard ceded it to Otho. Hence, from 1196 at least, about which date Otho appears to have held the title, Duke of Aquitaine is merely a courtesy title equivalent to Count of Poitou, and German historians refer to Otho as "the Poitevin". After Richard's death in 1199 Eleanor renewed her own title to the duchy by doing homage to Philippe for it: she then

gave Poitou to John as her heir, but received his homage
for it as count, a precaution which she doubtless took to
prevent the possibility of forfeiture to Philippe, the
suzerain. John, however, styled himself Duke of Aquitaine.
When Philippe in 1202 pronounced John's fiefs as forfeit to
himself, the legal position in Poitou was further obscured
by this action and any Poitevin noble might be excused
for wondering to whom his allegiance was due.[1]

There was the further fact that the inhabitants of the
land between the Loire and the Garonne had little in
common with the populations of Normandy and Brittany.
Under the dynasty of the Counts of Poitou, Aquitaine
had regarded itself as a feudal nationality. When that
dynasty ended and Queen Eleanor became its last re-
presentative, if unity was destroyed, antipathy to the
North was not diminished. The ideal of every territorial
lord was independence, and a determination to resist
foreign domination became the only basis of a common
policy. This resolve was intensified by the efforts of
France and England to secure possession of the province.
The cases of Normandy and Anjou were different. When
Philippe declared John a disobedient vassal, and his fief
as forfeit to himself, he gained the adherence of Norman
and Angevin barons, not only because they despised
John, but because they were becoming conscious of
affinities between themselves and the Frenchmen of
Philippe's dominions; language was no such obstacle as
it was between the Poitevin and the Parisian;[2] social life

---

[1] Stubbs, *Historical Introductions to the Rolls Series*, ed. Hassall, London,
1902, p. 455. In 1215 the position was changed: Reginald de Pons, a
noble of Saintonge, then became Seneschal of Poitou and Gascony in
conjunction and thereafter the two offices became one.

[2] Poitevin, so far as documentary evidence is available, shows some
affinities with Provençal but belongs to the northern dialects. Brunot,
Histoire de la Langue française, Paris, 1905, I, pp. 324–5.

and customs were similar. The case of Aquitaine was not the same; difference of language was a real barrier and society lived a different life. Hence the men of Aquitaine supported John against Philippe as they had fought for Richard against Henry II. Independence was their object, and fusion with Normandy and Anjou their aversion. John as a nominal overlord suited them admirably; he was too remote, too incompetent, and too short-sighted to interfere seriously with their ideals of regionalism.

A further complication was introduced by the increasing importance of the towns during this period. The development of the commune had improved the standard of living and increased the security of the workers and craftsmen who became more numerous as trade increased. Feudal lords were obliged to treat the towns with some consideration and could no longer disregard them in calculations of policy. A typical case is that of La Rochelle, which owed its rise to the protection of the Mauléon family, though marriages or conquests had transferred it to the Dukes of Aquitaine, to the Counts of Anjou or of Poitou from time to time. These overlords exacted various tolls and taxes which were a continual source of vexation to the inhabitants. When Henry II of England married Eleanor of Aquitaine, he claimed the town through his wife, and Ebles de Mauléon, who then regarded himself as the overlord, was obliged to give way. Henry realised that a mere change of suzerainty was not likely to content this mercantile centre, and therefore granted the town a new charter which was received with the greatest satisfaction. It was in part a confirmation of privileges already promised or acquired; the commune was recognised, the citizens were granted certain rights of administering justice, were allowed to construct fortifications and to defend themselves against any infringement of their privileges; taxes upon inheritance and other port and harbour duties were abolished. The town remained faithful to Henry during the revolt of his sons and was prepared to support John, until his selfish incompetence made their position impossible. John had confirmed the charter granted by Henry: the Mauléon family were to have the Talmondais and its revenues as compensation for abandoning any claims they had on La Rochelle.[1]

Savaric de Mauléon first appears in history in the year 1202 when he may have been some twenty-five or thirty years of age. John Lackland had followed Richard Cœur de Lion on the throne of England in 1199; Philippe Auguste of France supported the claims of John's nephew, Arthur of Brittany, and acknowledged him as heir to Normandy and Brittany over which he claimed feudal rights. War followed between Philippe and John, which was interrupted by the French king's matrimonial difficulties. He wished to divorce Inge-burge, the sister of Knud VI of Denmark, with whose hand he had acquired the shadowy rights to the crown of England which descended from Sven II, and which Philippe hoped would provide an excuse for repeating the conquest of 1066. Immediately after the marriage Philippe displayed an invincible antipathy for his bride,

---

[1] Four mentions of Raoul de Mauléon in 1200 suggest that he was in John's confidence; see Rot. Chart. I, pp. 58, 59: "Johannes etc. Radulpho de Maloleone seniori Pictavensi salutem. Mandamus vobis quod omnes feudos et terras quos dedimus bachellariis quos retinuimus de familia nostra in balliva vestra, qui homagium et fidelitates et ligentias nobis non fecerunt in manum nostram capiatis, donec aliud preceptum habueritis, nisi fidelitatem nostram et ligantiam [*sic*] jurare voluerint." (Feb. 3, 1200.)

and succeeded in getting a divorce pronounced by an assembly of French bishops and grandees, which Pope Innocent III refused to recognise. Eventually France was laid under an interdict and Philippe was obliged to make peace with John in 1200. Philippe's son Louis was to marry John's niece, Blanche of Castile; as her dowry, John was to cede certain lands to Philippe and to pay 20,000 marks as "rachat" (relief), in return for which he would be admitted heir to Richard's possessions; he was to do homage to Philippe and to receive the homage of Arthur for Brittany; in short John was to be relieved of any anxiety concerning Arthur's claims and to be recognised as Lord of Maine, Anjou and Aquitaine; he certainly lost a good line of defence for Normandy, but so astute a politician as his mother, Queen Eleanor, approved of the arrangement and helped to bring about the marriage. John then proceeded to upset the prospects of peace by a characteristic display of short-sighted selfishness. He had divorced his first wife and was considering the sister of the King of Portugal as a possibility, when he met in the course of a tour in Aquitaine Isabel,[1] the daughter of Adémar Count of Angoulême, and fell deeply in love with her. She was already betrothed to Hugh Le Brun the younger, of Lusignan, and as she married him after John's death, we may assume that her affections were already and permanently his. But John persuaded her father to hand her over and married her without delay at Angoulême. He thus estranged the formidable and ambitious house of Lusignan, the members of which had played an important part in Eastern affairs. The Lords

[1] Strònski, *La Légende amoureuse de Bertran de Born*, Paris, 1914, p. 82.

of Aquitaine appealed from their immediate suzerain, John, to their superior, the King of France. John was summoned before the court of his peers at Paris, but would not appear. The court passed sentence in 1202 and declared that John had forfeited the fiefs which he held from the King of France for disobedience to his overlord. War broke out again, as Philippe proceeded to enforce this decree, and Arthur was sent by the king with a small force to co-operate with the Lusignans in Poitou. John's chief supporter in this province was his mother, Queen Eleanor, and when the Lusignans heard that she was established in the castle of Mirebeau in Vienne with no great force, they induced Arthur to join them in attacking his own grandmother, whom they regarded as the chief support of John's power in Aquitaine. Savaric joined them with thirty knights and seventy men-at-arms. The town and outworks of the castle speedily fell into the hands of the besiegers and the queen was shut up in the keep. She had, however, contrived to send word of her danger to John, who was in any case on his way to Poitou with a force of Flemish mercenaries. He then received the message at Le Mans, some hundred miles from Mirebeau, on July 30; with unusual energy he pressed on his advance so rapidly that he reached the town in the early morning of August 1 and surprised the besiegers within their outworks. Among the prisoners were Arthur, Hugh Le Brun and Geoffrey of Lusignan his uncle, and Savaric de Mauléon.[1]

[1] R. Coggeshall, pp. 137–8; R. Wendover, pp. 168–9; Le Breton, *Gesta*, p. 76; *Philippis*, VI, ll. 250 ff. (in Bouquet, tom. XVIII); Meyer, *Le Maréchal*, III, pp. 165.

John distributed his prisoners among various castles in Normandy and England. Bertran, the son of the troubadour Bertran de Born, wrote a *sirventes* on these events which he dedicated to Savaric; the *razo* or prefatory explanation thus describes them:

John found them asleep and captured them all, Arthur and his barons and all those that he had with him. And for jealousy of his wife because he could not live without her, he abandoned Poitou and returned to Normandy and left the prisoners on oath or took hostages for them and crossed to England taking with him Arthur and Savaric de Mauléon and the viscount of Chastel Airaut. He had his nephew Arthur drowned, and Savaric de Mauléon he put into the tower of Corp, where there was never food nor drink, and the viscount of Chastel Airaut likewise. As soon as the king of France knew that king John had gone to England with his wife, he invaded Normandy with a great host and took all the land from him. And the barons of Poitou revolted and took from him all Poitou as far as La Rochelle. And Sir Savaric of Mauléon, as a bold and wise and generous man, contrived to escape from the prison and took the castle where he had been prisoner. And king John made peace with him so that he let him go and made him governor of all the land of Poitou and Gascony which he had not lost. And Sir Savaric went there and began war with all the enemies of king John and took from them all Poitou and Gascony. And the king stayed in England in his wife's chamber and sent no help in money or man to Savaric. Wherefore Bertran de Born the young, the son of Bertran de Born who made the other *sirventes*, on account of Savaric's needs and of the complaints about them made by all the people of Aquitaine and Poitou, made this *sirventes*, "when I see the season renewed".[1]

This *razo*, as usual with *razos*, provides statements that must be accepted with caution; but contemporary

[1] Stimming, *Bertran de Born*, Halle, 1892, p. 141.

testimony is so copious that verification in this case is possible. John treated his prisoners badly; some twenty-five are said to have been brought to Corfe, where most of them were starved to death. Savaric's companion in misfortune was Guillaume de la Rochefoucauld of Chatellerault in Vienne near Mirebeau, presumably mentioned as a relative of Savaric. The place of confinement is given as "la tor Corp", which Chabaneau identified with the castle of Cardiff; it is Corfe Castle in Dorset which John used as a state prison as well as a residence.[1] Nor did John finally abandon Normandy until December 5, 1203, when he crossed from Barfleur to Portsmouth.[2]

Savaric is said to have made his four guards drunk, to have knocked them on the head and to have released himself and some followers from their fetters; he then established himself in the "maistre-forterece", which John prepared to storm; but the mediation of Hubert Gautier, Archbishop of Canterbury, secured an agreement and Savaric was removed to France under an order dated August 20, 1203, issued at Verneuil, which also censured the castle constable, William of Blundville, for his inefficiency. Negotiations continued for some months; eventually Savaric undertook to serve the king and give hostages for his fidelity in return for his release. The hostages were his mother, Alix de Ré, his wife, Belle-Assez de Chantemerle and fourteen others;[3]

---

[1] See, *Dorset, Victoria County History*, II, p. 135 and references there given. See Appendix 3.

[2] R. Cogg. p. 146; Meyer, *Le Maréchal*, III, p. 170; Rot. Pat. I, p. 44 b; his hostages given under year 1205; *ibid.* p. 55 b; *Hist. des Ducs de Normandie*, p. 100.

[3] Rot. Pat. I, pp. 33 b, 37 b, 44 b, 55 b. See Appendix 4. July 28, 1205, 15 marks are paid to Alix, Rot. Claus. p. 44. J. E. Jolliffe, *Con-*

CORFE CASTLE TO-DAY

in the following years we meet with occasional letters ordering the transference of some of these hostages from one custodian to another. Orders were sent for the ship that brought them over to bring also two tuns of good wine,[1] in John's opinion, perhaps an equally important part of the cargo. Savaric was released in August 1204; on August 6, the treasury is ordered to pay him 200 marks; on the 10th, Robert of Turnham, the Seneschal of Poitou, is informed that Savaric is to have the lands which his father, Raoul, held on the day of King Richard's death.[2] This question of lands may have formed part of the terms of agreement; in any case, Savaric knew that he could not long hold out in the keep of Corfe. John was well aware that his affairs in Poitou were in a bad state; like other Plantagenets, he was a good judge of men and rightly considered that Savaric could be of more use to him alive and free than imprisoned or dead, and so sent him across the Channel in freedom.

While Savaric was in captivity John had lost Normandy and the French were in possession of Maine, Anjou and Touraine with the exception of one or two strongholds. In Poitou John's seneschal, Robert of Turnham, was struggling with Guillaume des Roches, the Lusignans and Savaric's uncle, Guillaume, and here Savaric was sent to support him. He recovered possession of Niort on May 1, 1205, by a stratagem

stitutional History of England, London, 1937, p. 250, notes that this is the first known agreement of the kind for bringing under obligation a foreign auxiliary who did not regard the king as his "natural lord": it became a model for John's exactions of hostages and special charters from his own vassals a few years later, in disregard of feudal convention or justice.

[1] Rot. Claus. p. 3.   [2] Ibid. pp. 5, 6.

which is thus described.[1] It was customary for the citizens of the town to go every year on May 1 to a neighbouring wood and to cut branches of may for the decoration of themselves and their houses. Savaric avoided any move upon the town until the day before this ceremony; then he ordered his troops to deck themselves with may, and marched into the town while the citizens were occupied in the wood. He found the castle undefended and was able to secure his position and take hostages for the good behaviour of the place. The king's supporters attacked Savaric without success, but by the autumn of 1204 John had lost all Poitou except Niort, Thouars and La Rochelle. The troubadour son of Bertran de Born advised Savaric that he would get little support from John:

> Savarics, reis cui cors sofranh
> Fara grieu bo envazimen,
> E puois a cor flac, recrezen,
> Ja mais nuls hom en el no ponh.[2]

Savaric, a king whose heart is weak will hardly conduct a good campaign, and as his heart is soft and recreant, no one ever puts trust in him.

John made some attempt to collect a force in England for service in Poitou but the opposition of the barons and the question of expense brought the attempt to nothing. By the end of June 1205 the French had captured Loches and Chinon, and made Robert of Turnham and Hubert de Burgh prisoners. Savaric was then appointed Seneschal of Poitou.[3]

The post of seneschal was no sinecure. His duties

---

[1] *Hist. des Ducs de Norm.* p. 101.
[2] Stimming, *Bertran de Born*, p. 144.
[3] Rot. Pat. I, pp. 49b, 53, 58a. See Appendix 5.

were to maintain the authority of his overlord, the king, to see that the royal dues and taxes were paid, to keep the peace and prevent nobles from quarrelling with one another and from oppressing the towns, and to carry out the king's orders as they came in. For so responsible a position discretion and tact were necessary, and much initiative power was allowed to the holder of it: "si id videritis esse commodum" and similar phrases recur in letters of instruction. During these years Savaric is required to settle various disputes about land tenure, to inquire for one Stephen of Alba Mara who may have been captured in war, and to get him ransomed; to settle the case of a captured warship; to put a reliable holder into the castle of Clisson and to take hostages for his fidelity; to provide one Robert of Bosc with money and land "where he can serve us"; to pay Regina of Pons 100 marks "owed by us" from the forest fiefs of Saintonge, "if you think this to our advantage and that she will not waste nor destroy the forest; if you think otherwise, give her the dues upon some other property"; to inquire whether the estate of Guillem Arnaut de Mote has been justly divided between his sons and to redress any injustice; to restore his lands to William Coc on his return to the royal service and to entrust him with the castle of Merhin; to see that La Rochelle pays 40 livres to Giraut de Camera, "until I assign him income from another source"; to investigate the case of two men, "who, says the Bishop of Saintonge, wish to return to our service; we have told the Bishop that we confirm his action, subject to your approval"; to send six tuns of wine which the Portsmouth authorities are to receive and forward. Add to these commissions a steady stream of local applications and complaints and it will be realised that the title of seneschal was by no means merely ornamental.[1]

On June 7, 1206, John arrived in La Rochelle with a considerable force. After three months of desultory warfare, a truce for two years to date from October 13 was agreed; John was to claim no lands nor allegiance north of the Loire and in other respects the *status quo* was to be maintained. Savaric and eleven others appear as signatories on behalf of John; on Philippe's side Savaric's uncle, Willelmus de Maloleone, appears.[2] John returned to England on November 4, leaving Savaric in charge of Poitou and Gascony.[3]

Before the expiration of the treaty, Philippe Auguste in 1207 attacked the Viscount of Thouars, who collected help from every possible quarter. A *sirventes* is extant in which the poet urges the need for supporting the cause of Thouars and appeals to Savaric.

> Savaris de malieon,
> Boens chiveliers a cuitainne,
> Se nos fals a ces besons
> Perdue avons nostre poinne.

Savaric, excellent jouster, if you fail us in this need, we have wasted our trouble.

John was fully occupied with affairs in England; but one chronicler states that the offensive was resumed at his command. In 1208 Savaric made a raid into Anjou, but Guillaume des Roches, who represented Philippe in Poitou, surprised and defeated John's supporters, capturing Hugh de Thouars, the brother of the Viscount

[1] Rot. Claus. pp. 53, 57, 61, 65, 72, 73, 82, 83, 87, 89, 93, 94, 101.
[2] Bouquet, xvii, p. 61 b; Rymer, *Foedera*, i, p. 95.
[3] Rot. Pat. i, pp. 66, 67.

Aimeric, and his son with other prisoners who were sent to Paris. Savaric escaped capture by flight, after vain attempts to rally the Poitevins.[1] Little of moment is recorded in the following two or three years of Poitevin history. On December 8, 1208, Savaric wrote to John from La Rochelle acknowledging receipt of 2200 silver marks, presumably part of the spoil which John collected in that year from the English church.[2]

From the beginning of the century, Southern France had been disturbed by the efforts of the Church to combat or to crush the Albigeois heresy. Pope Innocent III had been convinced by experience of the futility of peaceful persuasion, and by 1204 had resolved that force was the only remedy. He then urged Philippe Auguste to organise a crusade and promised liberal indulgence and absolution to all northern French nobles who should join. But the French king had already gained an indulgence as a crusader to the Holy Land and was fully occupied in consolidating his hold of the territories which he had gained from John of England. Innocent then applied to Pedro II of Aragon, promising him the possession of all land or property that he could conquer from the heretics. The chief of these in Innocent's opinion was Raimon VI of Toulouse; he was the most powerful among the vassals of the French crown and

[1] Le Roux de Lincy, *Chants Historiques*, Paris, 1841, I, p. 144; Wright, *Political Songs of England*, London, 1839; *Rigordus de Gestis Philippi*, Bouquet, XVII, p. 6; *Le Guillelmus Armoricus, ibid.* p. 82a and *Philippis*, VIII, ll. 290–300, *ibid.* p. 215c; *Chroniques de S. Denis, ibid.* p. 393e; *Chronicon Guillelmi de Nangis, ibid.* XX, p. 753b.

[2] Rot. Pat. I, p. 83 gave Savaric the right of striking a coinage. April 7, 1209, Poitou and Gascony are ordered to obey him, Rot. Pat. I, p. 90. Philippe Auguste visited him at Mauléon in May 1208 (L. Delisle, *Catalogue des actes de Philippe Auguste*, p. 252) : perhaps negotiations to detach him from John, conducted through his uncle, which came to nothing.

was in many respects almost an independent sovereign, claiming feudal powers over a large part of Southern France. He had married Jeanne, the daughter of Henry II of England, in 1196, the year after his accession to the county of Toulouse, and was thus the brother-in-law of John of England. Jeanne died in 1199; her eldest son, Raimon, eventually succeeded his father as Raimon VII, and her place was taken by Eleanor, the sister of Pedro II of Aragon, whom the Pope could hardly expect to attack his own brother-in-law. Raimon himself appears to have been an orthodox indifferentist, as were many nobles of his time and felt no interest in a church, the venality and corruption of which were obvious to all the world. The details of the heresy and the initial measures of the Pope need not concern us here. The murder of his legate, Pierre de Castelnau, on January 15, 1208, aroused excitement comparable only with that stirred up by the murder of Becket thirty-eight years previously, and the papacy took full advantage of it. The crusade began in 1202 and was carried on with every circumstance of cruelty and treachery until the crusaders had performed their forty days as required, when the force began to break up. Simon de Montfort became leader and undertook the difficult task of holding what had been gained with such forces as he could keep together. These varied greatly in quantity and quality and a stronger and more resolute man than Raimon of Toulouse might well have been able to save the situation. Raimon made a complete submission at the council of St Gilles in 1210, and hoped that he would be left in peace; but in the following year, de Montfort demanded possession of Toulouse. The citizens resolved

upon resistance and drove off the crusaders with considerable losses. Raimon was encouraged by this success
to begin an aggressive policy; he captured two castles and
then began the siege of Castelnaudary; at this moment
Savaric de Mauléon, whom he had already asked
for help,[1] came to his support, "with a fine company
of Gascons and others skilled and valiant; Savaric was
warmly welcomed by the count and the other lords, and
when all were mustered, they found that they had 2000
men capable and well armed."[2] It has been supposed[3]
with some probability that Savaric referred to this enterprise in a stanza which survives from a lost poem
addressed to Eleanor, the wife of Raimon VI of Toulouse.

> Dompna, be sai q'oimais fora razos
> qe, pois qe tot vos conqerun rauban,
> qe'us conqezes e be ai fait aitan
> c'aiostat n'ai Bascles e Bramanzos,
> la merce Deu, tan q'en be sem cinc cen,
> qe farem tot lo vostra mandamen,
> e mandatz nos la vostra volontat,
> c'ar montarem, qe tot avem celat.[4]

Lady, I know well that now it would be reasonable, since all
conquer you with their plundering, that I should conquer
you (from the robbers) and I have gone so far as to bring
together Basques and men of Brabant, thanks to God, so
that there are now five hundred of us who will all perform
your bidding, and send to tell us your wish, for now we will
get to horse, as we have kept the matter secret.

There were obvious reasons for Savaric's action;
Raimon of Toulouse was John's brother-in-law, and his

---

[1] P. Meyer, *Chanson de la Croisade*, l. 1424.

[2] *Histoire de la guerre des Albigeois* (prose version of the *Chanson*). Collection des Mémoires, VI, p. 78, *Chanson*, l. 1949.

[3] *Hist. Litt. de la France*, XVIII, p. 681.

[4] A. Kolsen, *Neuphilologus*, II, p. 147.

nephew, the young Raimon, was at a later date received in England from whence he was brought in 1215 to attend the fourth Lateran Council. Savaric's sympathies were naturally with the Southerners, whose language he spoke and wrote. As we shall see, he had also no intention of fighting at his own expense. While this is the first notice that we have of his intervention in the struggle, the violent language of the fanatical chronicler Pierre de Vaux-Cernay suggests that he had already made himself conspicuous: "with them came that wicked apostate, that prevaricator, that son of the devil in iniquity, the minister of Anti-Christ, Savaric de Mauléon, a heretic beyond all others worse than an infidel, insulter of the church and enemy of Jesus Christ....Oh, prince of apostasy, worker of cruelty, author of perversity, accomplice of the wicked!" Pierre does not hesitate to vilify the opponents of the crusaders, but this catalogue of maledictions is unusual, even for him. Raimon appeared under the walls of Castelnaudary about the end of September 1211. De Montfort had already shut himself up in the castle; the inhabitants readily handed over the town to the invaders, while de Montfort sent out messengers for help. Several of his supporters refused help or evaded the summons; at length de Montfort's marshal, Gui de Lévis, raised a small force which was increased by some 200 men under Bouchard de Marli and the Spanish adventurer, Martin Algai, and by contingents from the Bishops of Cahors and Castres. This force was intercepted by Raimon Roger the Count of Foix, as it advanced to Castelnaudary, and de Montfort, who was watching events from the castle, made a sortie to help them. Raimon Roger defeated the crusaders before de Montfort could arrive and his men then began to collect plunder; Bouchard de Marli contrived to rally some of the fugitives and attacked the disordered plunderers, while de Montfort's force fell upon them at the same moment; they were driven off the field and de Montfort returned to the castle of Castelnaudary. Here, Savaric de Mauléon had delivered an assault which failed; the author of the crusade poem says that this force wished to go back to Toulouse and abandon the enterprise; but Savaric persuaded them to defend their fortified camp:

> Savarigs crida'n aut: "senhors, estat tuit quei:
> No si move nulhs om ni pavalho no i plei,
> Que tuit seriatz mortz o vencut orendrei."

Sirs, be calm; let no one move nor fold his tent, or you will be all slain or conquered forthwith.

De Montfort soon abandoned the castle and went to raise fresh troops elsewhere.[1] This is the only occasion on which Savaric is mentioned as having fought for the Albigeois. In the following year, 1212, the Count of Toulouse is said to have met him at Bordeaux.

> E anc no i acabec lo valent d'un diner,
> Mas que cobre so filh e done gran aver.

and did not accomplish a penny worth of good, except that he recovered his son at great expense.

Savaric, unable to get his expenses from Raimon, had taken the young Raimon as a hostage, and demanded 10,000 livres as ransom.[2]

---

[1] Pierre de Vaux-Cernay, chaps. 56, 57; *Chanson de la Croisade*, ll. 1423, 1918–49, 2055–2219.

[2] See P. Meyer's note, *Chanson de la Croisade*, II, p. 142; *Hist. des Ducs de Norm.* p. 122.

This financial business ended Savaric's connection with the Albigenses. He also abandoned John, who was enraged at his method of extorting money from Raimon, and returned to the side of Philippe Auguste.[1] In July 1212 the French king promised him possession of La Rochelle, as a fief from himself, if Savaric conquered this and other English possessions in Poitou.[2] We next hear of him as a participant in the naval action of Damme. In April 1213 the French king held a grand council at Soissons, at which proposals were made for an invasion of England, the young Louis to be king of the country under the suzerainty of Philippe. This was a reply to the attempts of Otho of Saxony, the grandson of Eleanor of Aquitaine, to form a coalition against Philippe. A meeting was held at Valenciennes which John attended, but most of his continental supporters had abandoned him, and Ferrand or Ferdinand of Flanders was the only ruler willing to help the enterprise. The English fleet, however, destroyed the French shipping at the mouth of the Seine and at Fécamp, and averted the immediate danger of invasion. Philippe attacked the territory of John's remaining ally, Ferrand of Flanders, and sent a number of ships with supplies to Damme, formerly the seaport of Bruges. Savaric, who had attended the meeting at Soissons, was made commander of this flotilla for reasons not altogether complimentary to his naval experience.

> classem
> Praecipit ut properet Savaricus ducere Damum
> Pictonesque sui, quibus ars piratica nota est.[3]

---

[1] Rot. Pat. I, p. 92a.
[2] Petit-Dutaillis, p. 35 n.; Martène, *Collectio*, I, p. 1088.
[3] Walter of Coventry, II, p. 211; R. Wend. III, p. 257.

They appear to have justified their choice:

Pirata rapax Savaricus et ejus
Dira cohors,[1]

are said to have plundered merchant ships regardless of
treaties and to have exposed the fleet to hostile attacks
by their greed. Savaric held the island of Ré and a
stretch of coast from Châtelaillon to Olonne. Two ports,
La Claye and Savary, near La Rochelle, are said to
have provided depots for the proceeds of his piracy.[2]
Ferrand appealed to John for help; he sent a squadron
under his brother the Earl of Salisbury, who captured
or destroyed most of the French vessels on May 30.

In 1214 John was busy with preparations for bringing
into action his coalition against France, the centre of
which was his nephew, Otho IV, and which ended in the
battle of Bouvines. Ferrand of Flanders and William of
Holland joined him; a less useful ally was Raimon VI
of Toulouse who came to England at the end of 1213
after his defeat by de Montfort at Muret and, after
representations from the papal legate, was obliged to
return almost immediately. John collected a force of
mercenaries and a sum of 40,000 marks and arrived at
La Rochelle in the middle of February 1214. The Poitevin
nobles accepted his nominal suzerainty, and Savaric de
Mauléon made his peace with John through the good
offices of the Bishop of Bordeaux.[3] It may be that

---

[1] Le Breton, *Philippe*, pp. 293, 380. See *Hist. des Ducs de Norm.*
pp. 130 ff.; Meyer, *Le Maréchal*, III, p. 202; Ramsay, p. 441; Matthew
Paris, *Chron. Maj.* II, p. 549.

[2] Ledain, p. 21.

[3] Ramsay, pp. 449–50. Negotiations to this end seem to have been
going on for some time beforehand. John wrote to Savaric, Aug. 22,
1213: "Sciatis quod misimus in partes Pictaviae dilectos et fideles nostros

Savaric's behaviour at Damme had caused a breach between him and the French king. Moreover, Savaric's uncle died on February 27, 1214, and it is likely that Savaric wanted to secure his inheritance before rejoining John; his estates were now doubled in extent and he counted henceforward as one of the most powerful Poitevin barons. After some military operations John also received the homage of the Lusignans, Hugh Le Brun X, Count of La Marche, his son Hugh, Ralph, Count of Eu, and Geoffrey; an agreement was ratified at Parthenay on May 27. John promised his daughter Joan in marriage to the younger Hugh, the son of the man from whom he had taken her mother; the bride was not quite four years of age, but she would have a handsome dowry in lands, if John succeeded in conquering them, while her future husband was to be Seneschal of Saintonge and Oléron. Savaric appears as one of John's guarantors to this convention.[1] On June 20, John wrote to de Burgh, saying that Savaric was to have the house occupied by Walter Hasard in Angers. John was then besieging La Roche-aux-Moines, the fortress of Guillaume des Roches, Philippe's seneschal in Anjou, and we may suppose that Savaric had followed his somewhat

G. de Nevill camerarium nostrum, et Philippum de Albiniaco ad negotia nostra expedienda. Et, quoniam audivimus quod poenitet vos a servitio nostro, per consilium non sanum, et suggestionem sinistram, recessisse, unde plurimum gavisi sumus, eosdem ad vos mittimus, ut vobiscum super agendis nostris et vestris, et super hiis, quae nos et vos adinvicem contingunt, plenius tractatum habeant." Rymer, I, p. 114. The reconciliation was reported by John in a letter to William the Marshal, March 8, 1214, from La Rochelle: "Venit similiter ad voluntatem et misericordiam nostram Savaricus de Malo Leone, quem, consilio Domini Burdegalensis archiepiscopi et aliorum fidelium nostrorum, in pacem nostram admisimus." *Ibid.* p. 118.

[1] Rot. Pat. I, p. 198.

desultory campaign up to that point.[1] He was then sent by John to the help of Raimon of Toulouse, but was defeated by de Montfort;

> Pauci fugientes cum Savarico
> Quem rex Anglorum temere praefecerat illis
> Vix vitam salvare fuga meruere pudenda.[2]

John returned to England on October 15, 1214. The battle of Bouvines had wrecked his continental schemes, he had been defeated by Louis in Poitou, and had made an ignominious peace with France and a truce with the Lusignan party in Poitou, to which Savaric was one of the witnesses.[3] Savaric may have accompanied him on the return voyage; he was certainly in England shortly afterwards. On June 8, 1215, John issued a safe-conduct for the barons to meet him at Staines between June 9 and 11; this was extended to June 15, and notice of the extension was sent by John to his officers, in the list of whom Savaric stands second, a fact which suggests that he held a position of responsibility. Matthew Paris relates that John

bitterly grieving for the loss of his forty thousand marks, exclaimed; "after I was reconciled to God and submitted myself and my property to St Peter and the Church of Rome, no prosperity, but adversity only has fallen to my lot". To which a bystander replied: "not yet have you been reconciled to God, for you have given no satisfaction to those whom you have injured." And one on the other side said: "When did you hear from anyone or see any pagan or

---

[1] Rot. Claus. p. 167 b. The Latin is "apud Rupem Monachorum". Petit-Dutaillis (*Louis VIII*, p. 49) objects to the plural form, which is that adopted by the modern post-office.

[2] *Philippis*, VIII, 865 ff. The reference may be to the capture of the castle of Marmande. P. de Vaux-Cernay, chap. 79, says that it was garrisoned by John.

[3] Teulet, *Layette du Trésor des Chartes*, I, p. 405, no. 1033; Rymer, I, pp. 125, 129.

Christian king who of his own free will submitted to slavery? But you, who were the most free of kings, voluntarily placed yourself and your kingdom in perpetual slavery, that you might the more shamelessly overthrow men who are your natural subjects." And the man who made this remark was Savaric de Mauléon, who had no fear whatever of the king's despotic power.

The anecdote is in keeping with John's character, for he was superstitious enough to observe religious formalities, in the hope that they would bring good luck (for which reason he was buried in a monk's habit), and was even more avaricious than any Jew that he persecuted.[1] He had no intention of observing the provisions of Magna Carta nor of any other agreement, as is manifest from his preparations to meet the coming storm. He collected ships, enlisted mercenaries and called up money to pay them from his deposits in various monasteries. On January 21, 1215, he sent orders to the authorities in the counties upon the southern coast to make provision for Savaric and his men, who were expected by him to make a landing at some southern port. On February 8 he was informed that Savaric and his troops had arrived in Dublin and the Archbishop of Dublin was ordered to arrange for their transport to England.[2] On May 11 John wrote from Reading to the Bishop of Winchester, who was to send a confidential person to arrange for handing over "our castle of Winchester to Savaric for him to guard and therein to quarter our Poitevins". A letter of May 16 from Marlborough to Johannes de la Charité requires the immediate transference of the castle.[3] From Freemantle the King wrote on May 18 to

---

[1] Matt. Paris, *Hist. Angl.* II, p. 151.
[2] Rot. Claus. pp. 185, 187 b.   [3] Rot. Pat. I, pp. 135, 136 b.

the bailiffs of the forest of Southampton that Savaric
and Robert de Bareville were to be allowed to take wood
from the forest as they pleased for the purpose of
strengthening Winchester castle.[1] On May 14 the
Viscounts of Dorset and Somerset were informed that
John had given his beloved Savaric de Mauléon the
manors of Warham and Cranburn with their appurtenances.[2] Soon after midsummer other foreign contingents
began to arrive at Dover. John was at Dover from
September 1 to 19 and was accompanied by Savaric and
Hugh of Boves; on the 22nd he sent for a helmet and
breastplate which Savaric was keeping for him. Hugh
was sent over to Flanders to raise more troops, in spite
of the fact that he had been ordered to dismiss his
mercenaries in August.[3] The manors of Petersfield and
of Mapledurham in the parish of Buriton, Hampshire,
had been granted by John to Savaric on May 27; but in
October the latter was given to Roger de la Zouche.[4]
Possibly Savaric had been too busy to take possession.
He took part in the siege of Rochester in October and
November. John intended to collect his forces from
overseas and to march upon London; it was thus of
importance to him to secure Rochester castle, before
which he appeared on October 13. The citizens who had
manned the walls of the town, broke and fled at the first
assault; nearly a hundred knights and about fifty men-
at-arms were driven into the castle and prepared to
stand a siege under the command of William of Aubigny;
they had few provisions and set their hopes upon a

[1] Rot. Pat. I, p. 137b.   [2] Rot. Pat. I, p. 136.
[3] *Hist. des Ducs de Norm.* p. 153; Rot. Pat. I, pp. 143, 144.
[4] Rot. Claus. p. 213.

relieving force of barons, which never came. John broke down the bridge across the Medway and thus secured himself from any immediate attack; he pressed the siege vigorously, while his forces not thus occupied used the cathedral as a stable and ravaged the neighbouring districts of Kent. Every known device was employed against the town, but the garrison, who expected no mercy from John, fought heroically. A tremendous fire, fed by the carcasses of forty fat pigs, brought down the south-west tower of the keep, which, as can yet be seen, was replaced by a round tower out of harmony with the square towers at the other angles. The garrison surrendered on St Andrew's Day, when their last morsel of food was eaten. John proposed to hang all the leaders, but Savaric dissuaded him by pointing out that mercenaries would decline to serve in a war in which no quarter was given.[1] A grant of land was made to his engineer, Reyner, on November 10.[2]

Having thus secured possession of the southern counties, John determined to ravage the lands of the barons. He divided his forces; one army was to march through the Midlands northward; another, under the Earl of Salisbury, Falkes de Bréauté, Savaric and Walter Buck of Brabant, with their gangs of mercenaries, was to block the roads from London and to harry the eastern counties. These mercenary troops were one of the plagues of the period, and almost every chronicler refers to them in terms of horror as a collection of landless ruffians who feared not God neither regarded man. Mercenaries had been employed since the time of William the Conqueror; they were especially convenient

---

[1] R. Wend. III, p. 336; Matt. Paris, *Hist. Angl.* II, p. 165 and *Chron. Maj.* II, p. 626.　　　　[2] Rot. Claus. p. 235.

for service overseas, when the mobilisation of a native militia and a feudal army dislocated the life of the country and produced a force whose loyalty was not always reliable. The Low Countries were the chief source of supply and, as Bishop Stubbs has suggested, the nucleus of these bands may have been crusaders out of work "who had concluded their salvation and rid themselves of their conscience by the same service". But in the thirteenth century this element had disappeared; their numbers were recruited by the scum of society and by the children born of their promiscuous concubinage; they were united only by desire for plunder and by a precarious allegiance to some banished noble or ferocious ruffian who was able to maintain an ascendancy of terror. Walter Map compliments Henry II on keeping them out of England:

These heretics have gathered throngs of many thousands, the so-called Routiers (*Ruttae*), and, arming themselves from head to foot with hide and metal, sticks and swords, have reduced to ashes monasteries, farms and towns, and have violated women without distinction, saying from the depth of their hearts, there is no God. This sect arose in Brabant, taking the name Brabançon, for at first, sallying forth as robbers, they made for themselves a law against all laws. Soon there were associated with these in the breeding of sedition, fugitives, false clerks, runaway monks; and deserters of God of every sort joined their hideous assemblage. They have now multiplied so immeasureably, and the hosts of Leviathan have waxed so mighty that they reside in safety or wander through provinces and kingdoms amid the hatred of God and men.[1]

They were classed with heretics and were excommunicated by the Church, which was the first object of their outrages. These were the originals of the Free Com-

---

[1] *De Nugis Curialium*, Dist. I, xix.

panies of the next generation which were better organised and disciplined and often rested upon some basis of nationality, as did the Catalan Almugávares. Generally known abroad as Routiers, they have other names, such as Brigandi, Pilardi, Ruptarii, derived from their occupation; or names perhaps derived from a locality or leader, such as Cotarelli, Palearii, Asperes, Triaverdins. They should not be confused with the Ribauds, who were army camp-followers and hangers-on.[1] Savaric may have had some of these Routiers under his command, but no doubt the backbone of his force was composed of his own Poitevins. Of Buck or Buc, nothing seems to be known. Falkes (also Faukes, Fawkes, Fauques) was a person of some importance. John raised him from obscurity, knighted him and gave him a responsible post on the Welsh marches in 1207; he was a competent, energetic and loyal soldier, without bowels of mercy to his foes, autocratic and overbearing to his equals like many self-made men, but useful for an unpleasant piece of work, when prompt and vigorous action was needed. He became notorious under Henry III, when he and his brother held Bedford castle against the royal forces. Savaric seems to have been given or to have assumed the general direction of operations. On Christmas Eve, Savaric captured Pleshey, Geoffrey of Mandeville's castle; on Christmas Day, he plundered Tilty abbey during the celebration of mass, "overturned the furniture, broke open several chests, and carried off the deposits therein". On

---

[1] H. C. Lea, *Histoire de l'Inquisition* (French ed. Paris, 1903), p. 139, gives a number of twelfth-century references. For the Ribauds, see Meyer, *Chanson de la Croisade*, l. 400. In general, Stubbs, *Historical Introductions to the Rolls Series*, ed. Hassall, London 1902, p. 160.

January 1, 1216, he attacked the church of Coggeshall
and carried off 22 horses, the property of the Bishop of
London. Proceeding to Bury, he drove a number of
fugitives before him to the Isle of Ely. Winter had frozen
the marches and waterways and deprived Ely of its best
defence: the mercenaries broke in "and made a grievous
slaughter, sparing neither age, sex, rank nor religion:
they broke into churches and carried off their contents:
they tortured men horribly to get money out of them,
and the worst were the satellites of the aforesaid Buck".[1]
On January 29, 1216, Savaric began an attack on
Colchester, but retired to Bury on hearing that a relief
force was coming from London. Meanwhile John was
moving southwards; on March 3 he wrote from Hans-
lope ordering the constable of Norwich castle to give
Savaric free ingress and egress while he was on royal
service in Norfolk and Suffolk.[2] John reached Colchester
in the middle of March by way of Cambridge, Bury,
Framlingham and Ipswich. The castle of Framlingham
(and the lands) belonging to Roger Bigod were given to
Savaric who was there able to tell the king how Geoffrey
de Mandeville had been accidentally killed by a French
knight in a joust at London.[3] Savaric was then given
the lands of Geoffrey and of his brother William, with
the exception of the manors of Berkhamstead and Aile-
bury, a donation confirmed by Pope Honorius III on
September 21, 1216. Colchester surrendered in six days,
the French defenders being allowed to go to London,
while the English were held to ransom. John did not

[1] R. Cogg. pp. 179–80; Ramsay, pp. 490 ff. gives other references.
[2] Rot. Pat. I, p. 168.
[3] *Hist. des Ducs de Norm.* p. 165; Rot. Chart. p. 223; *Regesta Honorii Papae III*, Rome, 1888, I, p. 8, no. 37.

feel able to attack London, though he advanced in that direction; he turned aside at Enfield on April 1,[1] and went to Berkhamstead. Savaric, who had gone ahead to reconnoitre, was less cautious or less fortunate; he fell in with a London force, lost many of his men and was himself severely wounded.

Savaric apparently spent some time recovering from his wounds. Louis of France, who was connected with the Plantagenets by his marriage with Blanche of Castile, had been invited by the barons to take the throne; he landed in the Isle of Thanet on May 21 and the rest of the year is filled with his operations against John. He was received by the Londoners in June and advanced into Hampshire to attack John, who retired to Winchester on May 28. On June 7, Savaric was witness to a document under the style of Viscount of Southampton and warden of the castle of Porchester.[2] Louis reached Winchester on June 14; Savaric burned the suburbs and evacuated the town, leaving a strong garrison under one Godeschall of Malines in the castle, which Louis assaulted in vain until June 25, when Savaric returned empowered by John to negotiate a surrender on condition that the garrison should be allowed to withdraw.[3] John had retreated under

[1] At Enfield on this date John granted a quittance to the abbey of St Leodegar at Niort with certain market and hunting rights "ad petitionem dilecti et fidelis nostri Savarici de Malo Leone". Among the twelve witnesses who signed are Savaric himself and Hubert de Burgh. Rot. Chart. p. 220.

[2] Audiau, *Les Troubadours en Angleterre*, Paris, 1927, p. 26, gives a reference to MS. Harl. 86, j. 48 (Collectanea, ex rotulis in Archivis Turris London. temp. Joh. et H. III, membrane 70): "Savaricus de Malo Leone vicecomes Suthantonsensis Testis vii° Junii xviii° Regis. Et habuit castram Portestrum custodiendum." These two appointments were given to Savaric on June 5 and 7. Rot. Pat. 1, p. 186.

[3] Rot. Pat. 1, p. 188.

CORFE CASTLE IN 1643.

Savaric's persuasion on June 5 to Ludgershall, whence he retired to Corfe and thence to the Severn Valley, while Louis wasted time in the south-east.[1] On June 24 John wrote to Oliver and others in the castle of Wolves, saying that whatever Savaric should determine about retaining or surrendering Winchester, they at Wolves were to do the same. On July 3 a letter from Corfe to all castle constables and wardens ordered that Savaric should be received with royal honour when he came to a castle, whether his escort was great or small. On July 6 and 10 John informed Philip de Albianico that Savaric was to be associated with him in the command of the castle of Bristol; a letter from Oxford "to Savaric and his bailiffs at Bristol" concerning a quittance for 200 marks to the Templars seems to justify the inference that Savaric was then in sole command of the castle.[2]

John made an advance on September 1, when he moved from Chippenham, and declining battle, started on a tour of devastation through the eastern counties. By September 22 he was at Lincoln which became his base for a series of raids; Savaric accompanied him to Spalding and thence to Croyland, with the abbot of which John had quarrelled. John ordered him to burn the whole place and waited to see it done; a procession of barefooted monks with relics and an image of the Virgin persuaded Savaric to accept 50 marks and to leave them alone; but John was not satisfied until he had destroyed their winter's store of crops, which he burnt with his own hand.[3] John then moved to King's

---

[1] W. Cov. II, p. 229; Matt. Paris, *Chron. Maj.* II, 654.
[2] Rot. Pat. I, pp. 188, 190, 196.
[3] Matt. Paris, *Hist. Angl.* II, p. 189.

Lynn and gave Savaric command of the town which opened its gates to him on October 9, and was provisioned with some of the spoil from Croyland[1] whither Savaric had been ordered to return on September 30, "to seek and capture the enemies of the king who were hiding in secret places". John died at Newark on October 19; on the previous day he had sent a letter to Savaric[2] and it may be that the messenger who bore it brought a verbal summons to Newark. At any rate, Savaric was one of the witnesses to John's will[3] and was doubtless one of that grim escort of foreign mercenaries which carried the king's body from Newark to Worcester in accordance with his desire, and provided his soul with such safety as superstition could suggest, by laying the body dressed in a monk's habit between the shrines of St Oswald and St Wulfstan.

John's son, Henry III, was crowned at Gloucester on October 28; his two guardians, Gualo, the papal legate, and William the Marshal, Earl of Pembroke, took the chief parts in the ceremony, at which Savaric was present,[4] as also at the coronation banquet. The Marshal had been persuaded to undertake the governorship of the king and of the realm, in spite of his advanced years; Gualo summoned a council of the loyal prelates and

---

[1] R. Cogg. p. 183; R. Wend. III, p. 384; W. Cov. II, p. 232.

[2] Rot. Claus. p. 291: "Rex Savarico de Malo Leone salutem. Mittimus vobis trecentos Walenses qui pacati sunt de omnibus liberacionibus et areragiis suis usque ad diem Veneris proximum post festum Sancti Luce. Vobis mandamus quod ab illo die deinceps liberaciones suas eis habere faciatis. Teste me ipso apud Newercum xviii die Octobris." On the same day he wrote to the constable of Norwich: "Rex. Harveo Belet etc. Mandamus vobis quod fidem habeatis hiis que Savaricus de Malo Leone, W. comes Aubemarle et Falkes de Breauté vobis dicent ex parte nostra ad commodum et honorem nostrum." Rot. Pat. I, p. 199 b.

[3] See Appendix 6.   [4] Rolls Series, *Ann. Monast.* II, p. 286.

nobles to meet at Bristol on November 11. Savaric, as governor of Bristol castle, was naturally present; his duties as castle warden had been carried out in his absence by Hugh de Vivonne, who afterwards became Seneschal of Poitou. Savaric now asked permission from the Marshal to return to Poitou;[1] no doubt he wished to look after his affairs and estates; his position would be ambiguous, if Louis succeeded in establishing himself in England, and he may have already resolved to take part in the crusade. He seems to have obtained permission without difficulty; perhaps the Marshal had in mind those clauses of Magna Carta which demanded the repatriation of foreigners serving in England. On December 3 a royal letter was sent to him, stating that the abbot and monks of Tewkesbury were to have tithe from the town of Bristol as was customary and due "by the gift of our father John from the time when you took over the ward and custody of the town".[2] A further echo of Savaric's wardenship is heard on April 28, 1221, when the treasury is ordered to repay to the Bishop of Bath 25 livres which Savaric extorted (*extorsit*) at the time when he was constable of Bristol, "as appears from the letters patent of the said Savaric which he sent from thence to the Bishop himself".[3] Pope Honorius III apparently did not hear of John's death before December. On the 3rd of that month he wrote to his legate Gualo entrusting the young Henry III to his care and also sent a circular letter to several prelates and barons whom he considered likely to support the English crown: among these was Savaric, who was congratulated on his loyalty

[1] Meyer, *Le Maréchal*, III, p. 218.
[2] Rot. Claus. p. 294.   [3] *Ibid.* p. 454.

and urged to persevere in the same course.[1] It is likely that this letter arrived too late to influence Savaric's decision.

Savaric returned to Poitou at the end of 1216 or at the beginning of the next year, after an absence of some two years. He made large donations to the abbey of Talmond, to the priory of Saint Lambert, to the abbey of Fontenelles and to other religious foundations: his association with John had probably proved highly profitable, and he felt, as many more professional troubadours felt, that his spiritual safety should be properly insured. For this reason he resolved to join the undertaking generally known as the Fifth Crusade. The Fourth Crusade had been a failure, and Innocent III had begun the principle of using crusading ardour to attack heretics and infidels nearer home than the Holy Land, the Albigenses and the Moors in Spain. Few of the great men who might have led crusades were enthusiastic for such an undertaking: the prospects of securing principalities, estates and plunder were not what they had been. Yet throughout the thirteenth century crusades were planned, Europe was taxed to provide the necessary resources, and small expeditions and a trickle of pilgrims helped to sustain the tottering kingdom of Jerusalem. If the aristocracy was lukewarm, the common people had no doubt that crusading was a duty: but another Peter the Hermit, or another St Bernard, who might have concentrated and directed this enthusiasm was not forthcoming.

Innocent III had proposed a new crusade at the Lateran Council of 1215. He had died in the following

---

[1] *Regesta* I, p. 27, no. 143.

year and his successor, Honorius III, whatever his defects as a statesman, was a crusading enthusiast. He expended much time and energy in efforts to drive Frederick II of Sicily to redeem the pledge which he had made to Innocent III. When, therefore, Savaric proposed to support the undertaking, Honorius was ready to give him all possible assistance. He assigned a twentieth of the ecclesiastical revenues of Poitou towards the expenses of Savaric's expedition.[1] He also confirmed Savaric's privilege of striking his own coinage, and Savaric increased his ready money by mortgaging some of his estates.[2] The Italian merchants probably furnished equipment and supplies to be taken on board at Genoa. At a later date it was usual for the owner from whom the vessel was chartered to contract for the supply of food and service on board: in the time of St Louis the pilgrim's fare was a fixed sum.

Jean de Brienne, who had been appointed King of Jerusalem by Philippe Auguste and had taken possession of his kingdom in 1210, conceived a new plan for the recovery of the Holy City, when the efforts of Innocent III

[1] To the Bishop of Poitou, Guillaume Prevost: "cum dilectus filius nobilis vir Savaricus de Maloleone cum dilectis filiis Philippo Falcon, cive Romano, et Boncompagno Tornampollensi, Ragnucio Curtabrane, Aldebrandino et Spicinellio, mercatoribus Senensibus, debitum mille et ducentarum marcarum puri et fini argenti ad pondus Trecense contraxerit in ultramarino peregrinationis itinere constitutus, prout in ejus literis super hoc factis plenius continetur, ad nobilis ejusdem instantiam per apostolica scripta mandamus, quatenus, vicesimam eidem ab apostolica sede concessam et omnes redditus suos colligi faciens diligenter, te hiis ante omnia debita solvi facias debitum memoratum praefatis mercatoribus." July 6, 1219. (Bouquet, xix, p. 689.)

[2] D. Carpentier, *Supplément au Glossaire de Ducange*; Arcère, *Hist. de La Rochelle*, 1, p. 205; Ledain, p. 229. He mortgaged the île de Rhé, Châtelaillon, Benon and Bourt to Geoffroi de Neuville or Neville, Henry III's chamberlain, for 3027 livres tournois.

and of Honorius III had aroused Christendom to undertake the Fifth Crusade. He proposed to attack Egypt
and capture Cairo: success in this quarter would forthwith bring Jerusalem into the hands of the Franks. His
predecessor, Amaury II, had sent a raiding expedition
up the Nile in 1204, which had gone as far as Damietta,
plundering the neighbourhood and returning with considerable booty. The intention of Jean was to secure one
of the branches of the Nile by capturing Damietta and
so maintain his communications with his bases at Tyre
and Acre: after which the expedition would advance
upon Cairo. A start was made in May 1218 and within
a few days the Christian forces reached the neighbourhood of Damietta without encountering resistance. The
town was situated on the right bank of the eastern branch
of the Nile about two miles from the mouth of the river.
A mile and a half up stream was a canal which ran
to the sea and formed an island of the land opposite to
Damietta on the left bank of the river. Here the invaders established themselves. They were protected by
the river and the canal and their sea communications
were open: on the other hand, they were separated from
the town by the river, in the middle of which was a
tower commanding the situation and supporting a
system of chains by which navigation of the river was
blocked. The first task of the invaders was to capture the
tower: this was accomplished after much expenditure of
effort in August 1218. Operations then hung fire, owing
to dissensions among the commanders, and it was not
until February 1219 that the next general attack was
delivered. The Saracens had also been disorganised by
plots and cabals concerning a change of governors, and

the Christians were able to cross the river and invest the
town on both sides. The siege continued for several
months, in the course of which Savaric embarked his
crusaders, including the Count of Chester and some other
English, and sailed to Rome: from thence he went to
Genoa, where he met the main body of crusaders who
had come overland under the orders of the Count of
Nevers and Hugues de Lusignan. During September
Savaric arrived with these welcome reinforcements.
"Mas mosenher Savarix de Malleo era vengutz en l'ost
ab grans gens de pelegrins que bien nos ajudaron a
defendre."[1] On November 5 the defenders were so
weakened by death and disease that the Christians were
able to enter the town with no great difficulty. The
success caused great delight in the Christian world and
no less despondency among the Mohammedans. But
no permanent result was achieved. The Christians
quarrelled over the division of the spoils; intrigues for
the leadership caused dissension; and perhaps for these
reasons and because he felt that he had made his con-
tribution to the cause, Savaric returned to Poitou in
September 1220.

The French crown regarded the English dominions in
France as forfeited to themselves by John's action. This
claim was not acknowledged in England: Henry III
styled himself Duke of Normandy, Count of Anjou,
Count of Poitou and Duke of Aquitaine, and refused to
do homage to the French king for these fiefs. Much of

[1] P. Meyer, "La Prise de Damiette, relation inédite en provençal",
Bibliothèque de l'Ecole des Chartes, xxxviii (année 1877), pp. 497 ff.; Matt.
Paris, *Chron. Maj.* iii, p. 50: "Sed triumphator in Israel, omnipotens
Deus, castris suis providit, misso per mare Savarico de Maloleone cum
galeiis armatis et bellatoribus multis."

this territory was, in fact, already lost: Philippe had
conquered Normandy, Anjou and Touraine, and held
Poitiers: the rest of Poitou, which John had recovered in
1214, acknowledged the overlordship of Henry III. This
recognition was, however, rather nominal than real:
the feudal nobles and the communes in Poitou preferred
an absentee overlord to one who was on the spot, as
being less likely to interfere with their own freedom to
carry on their local feuds and to oppress the townspeople.
The province fell into a condition of complete disorder:
no seneschal was sufficiently strong to control the tur-
bulent barons, who expected to see the office confined
to one of their own order, but could not agree to support
any nominee. Such towns as Bordeaux, La Rochelle,
and Niort had grown in importance and population,
had obtained various privileges from the Plantagenets
and hoped to become independent municipal republics
under the protectorate of England. The obstacles to
these aspirations were the proximity of the French
monarchy and the aggressive and predatory policies of
the local nobility, whom the towns were by no means
able to dominate. The result was a maze of petty
quarrels and animosities for the threading of which the
modern historian has no sufficient information. The
general situation was, that England was too weak to
govern the province as a whole, and that if she espoused
the cause of either party, she was pretty certain to drive
the other into the arms of France. Under these circumstances few more unpleasant posts could be imagined
than the position of Seneschal of Poitou. Between
November 1216 and October 1221, when Savaric took
office, five seneschals had attempted to administer the

province. The situation was also complicated by the fact that the duchy of Aquitaine not only included Poitou and Gascony, but also claimed suzerainty over the counties of Angoulême, La Marche, Limoges and Périgord. Angoulême was the heritage of Isabel, Henry's mother, whom John had practically stolen from her affianced husband, Hugh of Lusignan, the son of Hugh, Count of La Marche. The Lusignan family was proud of its fame and importance. Two of the count's brothers had been crowned Kings of Jerusalem and Cyprus; another, by name Ralf, had become Count of Eu by marriage and owned estates in England. John had attempted to allay the anger which his marriage with Isabel had aroused by promising in 1214 her daughter Joan as wife to Hugh in place of her mother. In 1218 the count went to the crusade, and Hugh was therefore left in charge of the county. Joan was too young for marriage, but she was in Hugh's custody and he was officially regarded as Henry's brother; he claimed lands which John had promised him at the time of his betrothal, and in 1219 was trying to get possession of the estates of his uncle Ralf who died childless in that year. In 1218 Geoffrey de Neville was appointed seneschal; he had had some experience of the post in Gascony under John, and his difficulties are expounded in a series of his letters to Henry. In May 1219 he informed the king that Hugh of Lusignan was oppressing Niort, by way of prosecuting his claim to Ralf's estates, and that he declined to listen to any remonstrance. Neville declared that it was useless for him to remain and that he intended to start on the crusade (on which excuse two of his predecessors had resigned the post), unless Henry took better and more vigorous measures for the defence of his territory. In July he says that the barons are oppressing the townspeople and undermining their loyalty; "we are too poor to be able to defend the land or to subdue the barons, and they take no more account of me than if I were a pot-boy". Neville was so penniless that he could not afford to return to England; he therefore made a friend of Hugh and persuaded him in 1219 to become his surety for a loan of 160 marks advanced by some Rochelle merchants; Henry is asked to repay this sum. The messenger was one Bartholomew of Puy who had been mayor of Angoulême and had quarrelled with Isabel; she had occupied his land and taken his sons as hostages. Bartholomew, who had applied to the seneschal and to Hugh for redress, was on his way to England to prosecute his claim, and Neville suggested that the money should be paid to him; "and if Sir Hugh is obliged to pay it for me, you will never find anyone to make any further loan to your order nor to you". Neville also appears to have borrowed from the town of Dax.

Hugh had thus got Neville under his thumb and had made himself master of the situation. Henry or his council were obliged to acquiesce. In November 1219 both Bartholomew and Neville were in England, preferring their several complaints. A steady stream of complaints also came in from the towns; the local barons were holding burghers to ransom, commandeering animals and stopping field work. Could they have an efficient governor who would maintain the rights of the people and the interests of the crown? Early in 1220 news came from Damietta that the Count of La Marche was dead; in May Isabel of Angoulême informed her son that she proposed to marry Hugh; her daughter Joan was much too young for marriage and there was a possibility that Hugh might find a wife elsewhere and form connections detrimental to the integrity of the English provinces in France. Henry replied approving the marriage; but the union of La Marche and Angoulême, far from promoting peace and order, produced an even greater outbreak of disturbances.[1] Hugh pressed his claim for the restoration of Isabel's dowry by harassing the towns, and his example was followed by other barons, such as William Larchévêque of Parthenay. La Rochelle, Niort and Bordeaux implored the king "to send a strong man who will overcome the barons and restore the royal authority". Philip de Ulecote was appointed after much consideration by Hubert de Burgh, who knew from experience the difficulties of the situation; Philip died shortly after taking office and was succeeded by Hugh de Vivonne who lasted from January to October 1221. On the 6th of that month the prelates, barons and people of Poitou and Gascony were informed that Henry was entrusting these counties and their appurtenances to Savaric, and also that the sometime legate, Pandulf, now Bishop-elect of Norwich, was coming to inquire into the general situation. Savaric thus became in theory the supreme authority from the Loire to the Pyrenees.[2]

[1] Honorius III did what he could to support Henry's authority: on September 25, 1220, he issued a circular letter of congratulation to the nobles, clergy and people of Limoges, Saintonge, Niort, Périgord and other places, "pro defendendo Henrico rege Angliae contra eius matrem quae materni affectus oblita eum et terram suam facit indebite molestari." Savaric was one of the recipients. (*Regesta*, I, p. 452, no. 2727.)

[2] *Royal Letters of Henry III*, Rolls Series, I, pp. 30, 37, 44, 92, 126. A detailed account of affairs is given in Kate Norgate, *The Minority of Henry III*, pp. 130–45.

Pandulf's diplomatic mission had two purposes: to persuade the Count of La Marche to make a truce with Henry and to induce Savaric to undertake the responsibilities of seneschal. Savaric was obviously reluctant to accept the position. The English council were well aware that no more suitable man could be found; he was of high standing socially and politically in Poitou, with a considerable holding in the country; neither town nor noble could despise him as an upstart; he was a successful soldier of tried experience both in war and affairs; he had every interest in supporting the king's cause and was known to be an energetic and determined character. But Savaric knew that the house of Thouars, to which he belonged, was traditionally at enmity with the Counts of La Marche, and he was probably not surprised when Hugh, in 1223, theatened to withdraw his homage from Henry, if Savaric were not dismissed from his post.[1] He also saw that English difficulties in Aquitaine were largely due to want of money, and while he might count upon moral support, he felt that supplies of men and money were indispensable to success. The expenses of Pandulf's journey were met by a loan of 1000 marks from the city of La Rochelle, which the city of London was obliged to guarantee. He was commissioned on November 2

to bring about as best he could a prolonged truce between the King and the Count of La Marche and, having obtained this, to persuade and exhort Savaric de Mauléon to hasten into the presence of the King, who would (God willing) do what was right concerning Savaric's requests. If the bishop

[1] Petit-Dutaillis, p. 231; *Royal Letters*, I, p. 209; Rymer, I, pp. 159, 161, 166–9, shows the points of view both of the papacy and of Hugh.

elect of Norwich could not make a truce with the Count, then let him devote his diligence to the carrying on of the King's business according to decisions made in the King's presence; and let him deliver the care and custody of those parts to Savaric, inducing him thereto as best he could, and causing him to be efficiently provided with money for the defence of the land, according to the form which had been given him.[1]

Pandulf was successful in both objects; he persuaded Savaric to enter upon office and he concluded a treaty with the Count of La Marche which lasted until the following spring, when Isabel recovered her English dower-lands in April 1222. Early in the autumn of that year Savaric went to England for a conference with the royal council. He had had some ten months' experience of the difficulties in Aquitaine and doubtless wished to know to what extent he could count upon support from England. Representatives from La Rochelle, Niort, Bordeaux, the Viscount of Thouars and possibly from other places were present. La Rochelle had written previously complaining of the aggression of the Viscount of Thouars, stating that they had been obliged to come to an agreement with him and protesting their loyalty to Henry; Bordeaux had quarrelled with Savaric; the dispute was settled and the town was forbidden to form any federation with other towns without the royal permission; it was to restore tallages illegally levied and land illegally occupied, and to hand over to Savaric certain malefactors who had taken three castles and burned a bridge. Several letters patent to Poitou and Gascony order the inhabitants to receive Savaric with

---

[1] Norgate, *Minority of Henry III*, pp. 176, 177. Her emendation of the text of *Close Rolls*, i, p. 477 b is obviously correct.

confidence and respect, to pay to him arrears of taxation
and not to enter into unlicensed confederations. Savaric
is to resume all crown lands and castles wrongly
alienated; William Maingo and William of Mauzé are
to hand over their castles to Savaric, and the abbot and
chapter of St Sevère are to submit their charters to him.
The citizens of La Rochelle are ordered to construct a
new port "per consilium senescalli nostri Savarici de
Malo Leone", and are to raise the money by harbour
dues. In short the royal council realised that it now had
a competent and energetic seneschal and was prepared
to support him as far as it could; unfortunately, it was
support rather of a moral than of a material character.[1]

Meanwhile negotiations had been continued to secure
an agreement with Hugh of La Marche and Isabel; in
spite of papal threats of excommunication, they declined
to abate any part of their demands, and would concede
only a further truce to end on August 1. The situation
was changed by the death of Philippe Auguste, the King
of France, on July 14, 1223, and the accession of
Louis VIII. The royal council of England considered
that Louis was now bound to perform the promise to
which he had sworn when concluding the peace of 1217;
he then undertook to do his utmost to persuade his
father "to restore to the King of England all his rights
in the parts beyond the sea". The Pope was urged to
forbid the coronation of Louis until this promise had
been performed; letters patent were issued to the
nobles of Normandy, recalling them to their allegiance
to England; a fleet was concentrated at Portsmouth.

[1] *Royal Letters*, I, pp. 189–98, 200–6; *Close Rolls*, I, pp. 525–525b; *Pat.
Rolls*, I, p. 353; Norgate, p. 187.

But it was obviously dangerous to threaten Louis, if La
Marche and Angoulême remained sufficiently con-
tumacious to take his side; further efforts were therefore
made to pacify Hugh and Isabel, by giving them tem-
porary possession of two disputed towns until a final
agreement should be reached. Louis declined to consider the claim of the English crown and declared to an
embassy, which reached him on October 10, that not
only the continental possessions, but the English crown
were his by legal right. The treaty was to expire in
April 1224, and Louis would not consider any prolongation of it. It seemed likely that he would attack Henry's
remaining continental provinces; but nothing was done
to prepare for this contingency, except to conclude a
peace with Hugh of Lusignan by compensating Isabel
for her lost dower-lands in Normandy by grants of
English lands and allowing Hugh to keep most of the
places in dispute, with a generous indemnity payment
in cases where he waived his claim. Louis then offered
to prolong the truce for ten years, as he was anxious to
attack the Albigenses who had recovered much of the
ground lost in the "crusade", and had aroused the
alarm of the Pope. England would not agree to so long
a prolongation, and on May 15, 1224, Henry announced
that the truce with France was ended. He ordered the
seaports to prepare a fleet; but the only force sent to
La Rochelle was some hundred knights, under the
command of Richard de Gray and Geoffrey de Neville,
with a body of men-at-arms whose number is un-
specified; these troops went out early in June. Henry's
attention was concentrated upon the subjugation of
Falkes de Bréauté and the siege of Bedford castle during

the next two months, and within that time Poitou was
lost to him. Louis overbid Henry for the support of
Hugh de Lusignan and secured a treaty both with him
and with the Viscount of Thouars. On July 3 he attacked
Niort, which Savaric was holding and obliged him to
surrender the town: Savaric did not wish to lose La
Rochelle by defending a town, the inhabitants of which
considered that their municipal privileges would be
more secure under Louis than under Henry. On July 5
Savaric and his force were allowed to withdraw upon
conditions of offering no resistance except in La Rochelle
before All Saints' Day. There the seneschal might hope
for relief of help from overseas. It was a rich and well-
fortified port, of great strategic importance, as it commanded the whole seaboard, and could serve as a base
for operations on land.[1] As long as it held out, the
conquest of Poitou could never be completed. Louis
began the siege of La Rochelle on July 15, and met with
a vigorous defence. It is said that on the eighteenth day
of the siege a procession went to the abbey of St Antoine
to pray for victory, and that three queens took part in
the ceremony: Isemburge, the widow of Philippe,
Blanche, the wife of Louis, and Berengère, the wife of
King John of Jerusalem. Proposals for surrender were
received from Louis and rejected by Savaric, "prae-
fectus cujus intrabant tempora cani", according to
Nicholas de Braia, who credits him with forty hexa-
meters of patriotic exhortation of which the following
may serve as a specimen:

> Si tamen inter vos nimio terrore sepulti
> Et desperantes, sine bellis et sine nostri

[1] R. Wend. III, p. 84.

Sanguinis impensa censetis reddere villam,
Rectori nostro saltem legatio fiat,
Ipsi declarans nostrae discrimina sortis,
Nos extrema pati, nos pressos viribus hostis.
Sic nos posteritas a crimine proditionis
Absolvet, sic nos infamia nulla nigrabit.

The garrison, reinforced by the English knights, attacked the invaders with some success, but were finally driven into the city, which Louis began to besiege on July 15. The place surrendered on August 3; the garrison were allowed to march out with the honours of war and the citizens swore fealty to Louis on the 13th. Limoges and Périgord joined the conqueror, who was able to occupy Poitiers without difficulty. Louis returned to Paris in September, leaving a new seneschal behind him who was to join the Count of La Marche in an invasion of Gascony.

La Rochelle was lost for want of support from England. Henry made his struggle with Falkes de Bréauté the excuse for his neglect, when he explained his troubles to Pope Honorius III, and on this basis two preposterous fictions were erected. The Barnwell annalist whose work is incorporated in the chronicle of Walter of Coventry repeats a rumour that Falkes and Louis were acting in concert and that Falkes had promised to keep Henry fully occupied in England while the invasion of Poitou was proceeding. The only evidence for this assertion is Henry's statement to the Pope, "quae pericula imminentia nobis...praedicto Falcatio suisque complicibus non immerito debemus imputare".[1] In 1239 Henry brought a lengthy set of

---

[1] W. Cov. II, p. 253; *Royal Letters*, I, p. 226.

charges against Hubert de Burgh and accused him of losing La Rochelle by sending to the besieged boxes packed with stones and rubbish instead of the money that had been urgently requested; upon discovery of the fraud, the garrison went over to Louis in disgust.[1] Hubert denied sending any such consignment, and said that the town was lost because the citizens made peace with Louis without consulting the military authority; he then made the same reference to Falkes that Henry had made to the Pope. The fact was that Hubert and perhaps Henry had overestimated the importance of Falkes and had underestimated the danger to Poitou and La Rochelle, for the loss of which Savaric cannot be blamed. He had a composite garrison under his command: the Bordeaux contingent hated the Rochelais and both disliked the English. The Templars are said to have fomented this antagonism and Louis had probably bought various supporters in the town. The result was a quarrel between Savaric and his English troops, who are said to have formed the design of seizing Savaric's person; he, however, was informed in time and made his submission to Louis, considering that no reliance could be placed upon prospects of help from England.[2]

[1] Hubert's answers to these charges were noted by Laurence of St Albans whose MS. was preserved in the abbey and reproduced by Matthew Paris as "Responsiones Magistri Laurentii de S. Albano pro comite Kantiae Huberto de Burgo", Matt. Paris, *Chron. Maj.* vi, pp. 63–74; on p. 84, "optulit [Lodovicus] civibus non modicam pecuniam...at cives, cum a rege Anglorum se quasi derelictos reputarent, tam prece quam pretio tamquam nativi proditores inducti, regi Francorum sine aliqua controversia clam et subito Rupellam tradiderunt." See also Petit-Dutaillis, p. 245, and references there given. Thomas of Walsingham, p. 136, says that La Rochelle was lost "traditione Savarico, qui timens tantae proditionis poenas sibimet imminere, factus transfuga, ad regem Franciae se convertit".

[2] *Gesta Ludovici VIII*, in Bouquet, xvii, pp. 305 d, 307 c; R. Cogg. p. 208, gives "Galfridus de Nevilla, cubicularius regis" as the officer in

Louis thus gained possession of La Rochelle on August 3, 1224, and consequently of all the territory north of the Dordogne. Savaric was in a difficult position: he was unjustly accused of treason and he had every reason for regarding Henry's promises as unreliable. On Christmas Day in 1225 he swore to serve Louis, handed over certain castles as a pledge of his loyalty and was made governor or "warden" of La Rochelle, which had formerly been in the possession of his family, and also of the adjacent seaboard. He also became "custos partis maritimae", and was in command of the Isle of Ré in the following year, as Henry's uncle, William Longsword, the Earl of Salisbury, discovered, when he was wrecked there on his return voyage in November 1225.[1] Lusignan received the Isle of Oléron and undertook the business of conquering Gascony after Louis had returned to Paris. Fortunately

command of the English contingent, see Nicolas de Braia (Bouquet, XVII, p. 325, and the *Chroniques de Saint-Denis, ibid.* p. 419). The *Chronicon Guillelmi de Nangis* (*ibid.* XX, pp. 762 e–763 b) says that Savaric returned to England with the English contingent, and there discovered a conspiracy against him, whereupon he went back to France and joined Louis. The citizens of Bayonne took the opportunity of advertising to the king their share in the defence of La Rochelle and of blaming Savaric for the loss of it. "Your Highness has, we doubt not, received news of the surrender of La Rochelle to the King of France; it is said that it might have been defended, if Sir Savaric of Mauléon and the townsmen had been willing to show due fidelity to yourself. There were present some 400 of our citizens as men at arms, who were ready loyally to offer what help they could, as you will have learnt from your advisers on the spot. We were also about to send more of our best soldiers with ships and galleys, prepared at great expense. But the citizens of La Rochelle posted our men at the weakest part of the town, and they fled to their ships, when the citizens of La Rochelle let in the men of the French King without their knowledge." They are prepared to continue harassing the enemy, but apart from the expense of this, they have difficulties with the Kings of Castile and Navarre and cannot support the burden; they would welcome "succursum vestrae pecuniae", which request seems to have been the real point of the letter. Rymer, I, p. 173.

[1] Matt. Paris, *Chron. Maj.* III, p. 96; Petit-Dutaillis, p. 255.

for Henry, Bordeaux remained obstinately loyal, as its trade with England was far too valuable to be lost, and declined to make any kind of truce with Hugh of Lusignan, who was obliged to withdraw to his own province in October 1224. In the previous month Hugh of Vivonne reported that what Henry had lost could be easily regained; an archdeacon writing about the same time repeated the assertion of the citizens of Bordeaux that all they needed for success was money, "si pecuniam haberent, omnes inimicos vestros confunderent"; he considered that they could make good their words, if the king or his brother Richard were with them and "some good man to control expenditure".[1] Henry made his brother Duke of Cornwall and Count of Poitou in February 1225; in March he sailed for Bordeaux with his uncle, Earl William of Salisbury, Philip d'Aubigné and others. The expedition overran the country nearly as easily as Louis had done, but little reliance was to be placed upon the allegiance extorted from the local nobility. Savaric's fleet commanded the Bay of Biscay, disturbed communications and caused much dislocation of trade and commerce.

When the treaty between them had been denounced, the two kings agreed to allow merchants to carry on their commerce until July 9, 1224: notice of this arrangement was sent to Savaric by Henry on June 14: individual safe-conducts are said to have been granted to merchants in the Norman towns. But Hubert de Burgh took measures to stop all trade with La Rochelle: on August 23, 1224, he ordered the seizure of all ships arriving from Poitou; French merchants were arrested

[1] *Royal Letters*, I, pp. 237–9.

in English ports and fairs and imprisoned with few exceptions, while exportation to France was forbidden. The English trade with La Rochelle was forthwith transferred to Bordeaux, and Savaric proceeded to harass the English mercantile marine whenever he saw an opportunity. At the end of 1225 an English fleet carrying money to Richard of Cornwall for the expenses of his expedition in Gascony was becalmed off La Rochelle. Savaric ordered the ships into harbour, but a fortunate shift of wind enabled them to escape.[1] On March 23, 1226, Henry notified the barons of the Cinque Ports that "Savaricus de Malo Leone et quidam alii nobis malevoli et inimici" were becoming a serious menace to the safety of English cargoes, and urged them to consider the situation and inform him of their proposals.

Various intrigues were set on foot by Henry to strengthen his position. Among others, Peter Mauclerc, Count of Brittany, was attracted to the English cause by the prospect of a marriage between Henry and his daughter Iolande, and by a promise that his earldom of Richmond should be restored to him; Henry also promised an alliance with Raimon VII of Toulouse, his first cousin. The Pope Honorius succeeded in persuading Louis to lead a crusade against the heretical Raimon in 1226, and Savaric's name appears in the lists of the crusaders as present at the preliminary general meeting held in Paris on January 28. On January 8, Honorius had issued a circular letter to Hugh and Geoffrey of Lusignan, the Viscount of Limoges, Savaric de Mauléon, Hugh of Thouars, William Maingo and Geoffrey Rudel, re-

[1] *Ann. Monast.* III, p. 98; Petit-Dutaillis, pp. 257–9.

calling them to allegiance to Henry III.[1] In the course of the expedition Louis died, on November 8, leaving his throne to his little son, Louis IX, under the regency of his widow, Blanche of Castile. About the end of the year the Poitevin barons, including Savaric, made treaties with Richard of Cornwall which provided valuable concessions as the price of their support.[2] But early in 1227 Blanche was able to send an army south of the Loire, and the Poitevins reverted to their French allegiance. Peter of Brittany also abandoned his arrangement with Henry. Richard of Cornwall threw up the enterprise in disgust in April, returned to England with Savaric,[3] and left Poitou to the unreliable local barons, after making a truce with Louis IX, which Savaric[4] signed on behalf of "Richard, Count of Poitou". Rudel de Blaya, a descendant of the well-known troubadour, also appears among the signatories. Savaric's interests were protected under the terms of this truce; citizens of French or English suzerainty were to remain in possession of their property, "ita tamen quod mobilia quae ejecta fuerint de terra domini Sauvarici de Malloleone, per eos qui tempore piae recordationis dicti Ludovici Regis Francorum, relicta terra domini Savarici, apud

---

[1] *Regesta*, II, p. 393, no. 5776.

[2] "Regno etenim Franciae sic in manu mulieris et pueri derelicto Savaricus de Malo-leone et alii, consilio, sicuti dicebatur, magnatum Pictaviae, nulli ordini, sexui vel aetati parcentes, quaecumque terra ac mari capere poterant, rapiebant; in tantum se Regi Angliae submittentes quod Richardum fratrem ejus ad Rupellam aliamque terram Regis Franciae destruendam in auxilium vocaverant." *Ex Chronico Turonensi*, Bouquet, XVII, p. 318.

[3] *Ann. Monast.* I, p. 70.

[4] Savaric was warden of Carisbrook castle in 1227, *Cal. Pat.* 1216–1225, p. 129. If this is so, he retained his allegiance to England longer than any other of the Poitevins.

Rupellam sibi fecerint mansionem in dicta foeda reportabuntur". This stipulation seems not to have been
observed; Henry wrote to Louis, on October 10, 1227,
"our beloved and loyal Savaric de Mauléon, who was
one of our subjects at the time when the aforementioned
truces were agreed, as your serenity is aware, has come
to us complaining that your officers have despoiled him
of certain lands, rents and possessions, of which he was
in peaceful occupation before the truces"; he trusts that
Louis will amend this wrong and offers reciprocal action
in the case of French subjects.[1]

By the middle of 1229 the Bretons and the Poitevins
were again at variance with Blanche, and Henry received invitations to intervene in French affairs. Peter
of Brittany came over to Portsmouth in October and
did homage to Henry as King of France for the titles of
Earl of Richmond and Duke of Brittany. In May 1230
an expedition set out for St Malo, which eventually
entered Poitou only to find that the barons had again
changed sides and were supporting the French throne,
so that Henry's mother, as a Lusignan, was one of his
enemies. The expedition produced no decisive result.
In the expedition of 1230 Geoffrey of Lusignan and
others were captured by Henry and released upon doing
homage and surrendering territory or castles. One of
these was Herneus de Volurio, whose overlord was
Savaric. Herneus took the oath of homage to Henry
under penalty of losing his lands, if he should break his
oath, Savaric's assent having been obtained to this
arrangement, "salvo ipsi Savarico domino meo, et
haeredibus suis servitio, de praedictis terris eis debito".[2]

---

[1] Rymer, I, pp. 186, 187.   [2] *Ibid.*, p. 197.

In this year Savaric negotiated an alliance between Henry III and Peter Mauclerc of Brittany. Henry returned to England in October and in July 1231 a three years' truce was concluded between France, Brittany and England.

About this year 1230 may be dated a notice of Savaric which is given by the troubadour Peire Bremon Ricas Novas[1] who says of Sordello,

> mais dels autres dos ac qan venc d'Espaigna rics
> et apres en Peitau cum dav' En Savaric.

Il revint riche d'Espagne et il poussa jusqu'en Poitou au temps où "donnait" le seigneur Savaric.[2]

Savaric must have been one of the last nobles in France to keep a court to which troubadours were attracted by the generosity of the patron.[3] He is said to have broken with Louis IX and to have rejoined Henry shortly after the peace of 1231. In 1228 and 1229 he founded a Dominican convent at Fontenay, compensated the priory of Fontaine in Talmondais for damages and granted certain rights to the abbey of Orbetier at St Nicolas-de-la-Tranche. By a deed of donation dated 1226 he announced his marriage to his second wife,

---

[1] Ed. Boutière, Toulouse, 1930, p. 70, repeating Jeanroy-Bertoni, *Annales du Midi*, XVIII, p. 294.

[2] So de Lollis, *Sordello*, Halle, 1896, p. 26.

[3] A *partimen* between Albert de Sisteron and an unknown monk, probably composed within Savaric's lifetime, debates the respective merits of Catalans (Provençals) and French and states that a living cannot be made in France or Poitou.

> "E podetz ben, en Peitau o en Fransa
> morir de fam, s'en convit vos fiatz."

"You may well die of hunger in Poitou or in France, if you trust in hospitality." The monk, in the next stanza, defends the "Peitavis honratz" against this charge, which, however, must have been in circulation for Albert to have made it. (Appel, *Chrestomathie*, no. 97.)

Amabilis du Bois, and granted her rights in Châtelaillon, Benon, the Isle of Ré and other places; in 1227 he executed a deed declaring his marriage, before the Abbé of Orbetier, and ordered his vassals to recognise Raoul, the issue of this marriage, as his heir. This unusual proceeding suggests that the validity of the marriage and the legitimacy of Raoul were open to doubt; Raoul is said to have been legitimised on May 10, 1232, by the King of England and the Archbishop of Bordeaux.[1] The date of Savaric's death is doubtful; Ledain says that he signed in May 1233 a charter confirming the abbey of Luçon in possession of certain lands, died on July 29 of that year and was buried in the choir of the church of St Michel-en-l'Erm, one of the many religious foundations which he had supported. But Torraca notes a letter of Gregory IX dated November 27, 1231, forbidding the Archbishop of Bordeaux to decide a quarrel between Alice, the daughter of Savaric, and her husband on one side, against Raoul, the natural son of Savaric, on the other, concerning their father's inheritance, whence it may be presumed that Savaric was dead before this date.[2] Savaric founded or endowed some seventeen ecclesiastical establishments during his lifetime in or near to his own territorial holdings. He had also been granted the right

[1] Ledain, p. 295.

[2] Ledain, p. 362, refers to *Chronicon Alberici trium fontium* in *Hist. de France*, XXI, p. 607, *Hist. de Fontenay* by Fillon, p. 23, *Hist. de l'abbaye de Saint-Michel-en-l'Erm*, by Brochet, p. 14. For F. Torraca, see *Les Annales du Midi*, XIII, p. 530. In the royal *recepta et expensa* for March 25, 1233, appears the item "duo mercatores Hispani qui fuerunt spoliati per Savaricum de Malo-leone, eodem die, xx. l., teste domino J. de Bello Monte" (Bouquet, XXI, p. 233). This probably refers to some case that occurred during the disturbances of 1229–30, for which compensation was delayed.

of striking his own coinage on September 22, 1214,[1] and his coins were certainly in circulation in 1215. On May 27 of that year John informed the authorities of

Poitou, Angoulême and Gascony that Savaric's coinage was to be regarded as legal tender, as long as it had the same weight and alloy as Poitevin currency.[2] This privilege was extended on August 31; Savaric and his heirs were to have the right in perpetuity of striking coinage equivalent to tournois and of circulating it throughout Aquitaine.[3] These coins were generally known as "savaris". John confirmed this order by writing from Rochester November 6 and 12, 1215,[4] to Renaud de Pons, his seneschal in Poitou, and on September 14, to the mayors and notables of Bordeaux, Niort, La Rochelle and St Jean-d'Angely, ordering that Savaric's coinage, if of silver, should circulate at the same rate as the local currency.[5] The privilege was confirmed by Pope Honorius III on April 20, 1218, when Savaric took the cross.[6] Three types of coinage are known; a silver

---

[1] Rot. Chart. p. 200.   [2] Rot. Pat. 1, p. 141 b.

[3] *Ibid.* p. 154.   [4] *Ibid.* pp. 158, 159.

[5] *Ibid.* p. 197.

[6] *Regesta*, 1, p. 205, no. 1243.

denier, inscribed Savaricus (obv.) and Metalo (rev.); a copper denier, Jhesus (obv.) and MS LEO CIVI (rev.) surrounding three crosses; and the same, with the letter A added to the crosses. It is likely that the last type was struck by Amabilis, Savaric's second wife, when she inherited after his death.[1]

[1] De la Fontenelle, "Savaric de Mauléon", *Revue Anglo-française*, 2me série, II, pp. 309 ff.

II
THE TROUBADOUR
*

THE COURT OF POITIERS had been for some sixty years one of the most brilliant in Europe, and a famous centre of troubadour poetry, in spite of the fact that the Poitevin dialect cannot be assigned to the dialects of Southern France known collectively as Provençal. William IX (1086–1127) was the first troubadour known to us and the traditions of his reign were continued by William X (1127–1137), who was the patron of Marcabru and Cercamon. His daughter Eleanor befriended Bernard de Ventadorn and her tastes were those of her second husband, Henry II of England, who, like his father, was a patron of the arts and enjoyed the pleasures of an animated and lively court. His sons, the "Young King" Henry, Richard Cœur de Lion and Geoffrey of Brittany, were constantly held up to more decadent generations as models of knightly generosity to troubadours. But in 1198 the county of Poitiers fell to a German prince, Otho of Brunswick, and in 1201 to John Lackland who came to it only for the purpose of conducting campaigns more or less disastrous. The seneschals who represented him at Poitiers seem to have taken no interest in poetry, and possibly the only centre in the province at which troubadour or jongleur could find a welcome and obtain a hearing was the court of Savaric de Mauléon.

Savaric was a patron of the troubadour Jausbert de Puycibot, whose biographer stated that he was brought up in the monastery of "Sain Leonard", probably as his editor[1] supposes, the Cistercian house of Saint Léonard-des-Chaumes, near La Rochelle; Savaric was

[1] W. P. Shephard, *Jausbert de Puycibot*, Paris, 1924 (Les Classiques français du Moyen-Age).

a benefactor of this monastery in which Jausbert is said to have "learnt letters and to sing and compose well. He left the monastery at the will of a lady and came to him to whom all came who desired honour and kindness in courtesy, to Sir Savaric de Mauléon, and he gave him the equipment of a joglar and dress and a horse." Jausbert then in the course of his travels fell in love with a "Donzella gentil e bella" who declined to marry him unless he became a knight. Savaric conferred this honour upon him and gave him lands. Subsequently, says the biographer, Jausbert's wife was seduced by an English knight, while he himself was absent in Spain, and was finally abandoned and forced to make a living by prostitution, in which circumstances Jausbert discovered her by chance. The latter story is probably an invention by the biographer to explain the allusions to feminine deceit in two of Jausbert's songs; but there is nothing to disprove the account of Savaric's benevolence which is supported by three references to his generosity in Jausbert's songs:

> Senhe·N Savaric, larc e bo
> Vos troba hom tota sazo
> Que·l vostre ric fag son prezan
> E.l dig cortes e benestan.

Sir Savaric, one finds you always generous and kind, for your deeds are praiseworthy and your words are courteous and gracious.[1]

Savaric's poems have disappeared with the exception of his share in two *jeux-partis* and of one isolated stanza. It is not possible to assign dates with any certainty to these compositions. The term *tenso* denoted in general a

---

[1] Shephard, no. ix, l. 41.

poem in which a discussion was carried on by two inter-locutors in free style; when one of them proposed a choice between alternative propositions and allowed his adversary to choose which he would defend, the piece was known as a *partimen* or *joc partit*. The decision was usually referred to an arbitrator. This society amusement does not appear in Provençal literature earlier than the last years of the twelfth century, and a *partimen* with more than two disputants is unusual. The circumstances which suggested them are explained in *razos*, one of which the troubadour Uc de Saint-Circ says that he wrote and he was probably the author of the other. He was a close friend of Savaric, as will be seen later. The occasion of the first *tenso* is related as follows:

Sir Savaric of Mauléon had come to Benauges (Gironde) to see the viscountess, my lady Guilhelma, and he fell in love with her; and he took with him Sir Elias Rudel, Lord of Bergerac (Dordogne) and Jaufre Rudel of Blaye.[1] All three asked for her love and before this occasion she had taken each of them as her knight, and none of them knew that the other had been accepted. All three were seated near her, one on each side and the third in front of her. Each of them looked at her lovingly. And being the boldest lady that ever was seen she began to look lovingly at Jaufre Rudel of Blaye, for he was sitting before her; she took the hand of Elias Rudel of Bergerac and pressed it very lovingly; and with a smile and a sigh she pressed the foot of my lord Sir Savaric.

---

[1] Not the troubadour, whose well-known adventures and death took place in 1161-2, according to Stimming, *Jaufre Rudel*, Berlin, 1873, pp. 15-16. This Jaufre, with Savaric and Geoffrey de Pons, was guarantor to the truce made in April 1227 between the King of France and Richard, brother of Henry III and Count of Poitou: see J. Anglade, *Rigaut de Barbezieux*, Montpellier, 1919, pp. 23-4. Elias Rudel did homage in 1224 to Louis VIII for Bergerac and other fiefs (Chabaneau, p. 47 n.). His relation to the Counts of Périgord is obscure: see Stronski, *La Légende amoureuse de Bertran de Born*, Paris, 1914, pp. 122-3 n.

None knew the pleasure that the others had until they came away, when Sir Jaufre Rudel told Sir Savaric how the lady had looked at him and Sir Elias told about the hand. And Sir Savaric when he heard that she had given each of them such pleasure, was grieved, and he did not speak of what she had done to him, but called Gaucelm Faidit and Uc de la Bacalaria and asked them in a stanza to which one she had given most pleasure and love. And the question stanza began thus:[1]

I. *Savaric de Mauléon*: Gaucelm, I propose to you and to Sir Hugo three diversions on the theme of love; let each of you take the better one and leave me whichever you prefer. A lady has three admirers and their love so constrains her that, when all three are before her, she makes a show of love to each of them. Upon one she looks lovingly; another's hand she gently presses, and with a smile she treads upon the foot of the third. The case being thus, say, to which of the three does she show most love?

II. *Gaucelm Faidit*: Sir Savaric, be sure that that friend received the fairest gift on whom her fair eyes rested frankly without deceit. From the heart rises that sweetness and is therefore an honour a hundredfold greater. As regards the holding of the hand, I say that there is neither advantage nor loss therein, for ladies commonly accord that pleasure by way of welcome. And as for treading of the foot, I do not think that the lady did it as a sign of love nor should it be so interpreted.

III. *Uc de la Bacalaria*: Gaucelm, you say what pleases you, but you do not support what is reasonable, for I see no advantage as you argue, to the friend in being looked at; and if he thus understands it, it is foolishness, for eyes look on him and on others and have no other power. But when the white ungloved hand gently presses the friend's hand, love proceeds from the heart and mind. And let Sir Savaric, as he so kindly proposes, defend the courteous treading of the foot, for I will never support it.

IV. *Savaric de Mauléon*: Sirs, since you leave the best to me, I will maintain it without refusal. I say then that the

---

[1] See Appendix 7 for text.

foot tread which was given was a sign of pure affection, hidden from the eye of the slanderer, and this is clear, since the friend received this comfort accompanied with a smile, so that love is without deception. And if anyone regards the holding of the hand as a sign of greater love, he shows lack of sense. And I do not think that Sir Gaucelm would take the look as a better sign, if he knew as much of love as he says.

V. *Gaucelm Faidit*: Sirs, you who criticise the glance of the eyes and their pleasing way, do not know that they are the messengers of the heart which has sent it to them; for the eyes reveal to the lover that which fear retains in the heart, wherefore they do all the pleasure of love. And often with a mocking smile a lady may tread on the foot of many a one without other intent. And Sir Hugo argues falsely, for holding a hand is nothing and I do not think that it was ever inspired by love.

VI. *Uc de la Bacalaria*: Gaucelm, you and the lord of Malleo speak against love, and the dispute clearly shows that the eyes which you have chosen and for which you argue as the best have betrayed many lovers. And if the lady with a faithless heart were to tread on my foot for a year, I should not have a joyous heart. And as concerns the hand, there can be no dispute that its pressure is worth a hundred times more, for if it had not pleased the heart, love would not have sent it to the hand.

VII. *Savaric de Mauléon*: You and Hugo are certainly defeated in the dispute, and I should like my Gardacors, who has conquered me, to judge the case and Lady Maria, with whom is virtue.

VIII. *Gaucelm Faidit*: Sir, I am by no means conquered as will appear at the judgement, wherefore I should like Lady Guilhelma of Benauges to be there with her courteous loving speech.

IX. *Uc de la Bacalaria*: Gaucelm, I have such strong reasons that I overcome you both and defend myself, and I know a cheerful, pleasant lady in whose hands the judgement should be placed, but I do not see advantage in more than three.

The Maria proposed by Savaric was Maria of Ventadorn; she was one of the "three sisters of Turenne",
married Eble V of Ventadorn about 1190, and died
after 1221.[1] She was of high reputation in the society of
her time and was also a *trobairitz* who took part in a
tenso with Gui d'Ussel.[2] Gardacors is the *senhal* for
Guilhelma de Benauges, the wife of Peire de Gavaret,
Viscount of Benauges,[3] one of whose poems has survived.
Maria of Ventadorn was the love of Gaucelm Faidit;
perhaps he and Savaric compliment one another by
nominating each other's ladies; in any case Uc de la
Bacalaria is taken in, as he fails to identify Gardacors
with Guilhelma and hence supposes that three arbi-
trators have been proposed.

It was probably after Savaric had been made
Seneschal of Poitou in 1205 that he came into close
relations with troubadours and the courts which they
frequented. After 1213, his life seems to have been too
preoccupied with politics and war to leave much time
for poetry. Three of the troubadours with whom his
name is associated were Limousins. Gaucelm Faidit,
who belonged to Uzerche (Corrèze), is represented by
some seventy poems, of which perhaps the best known
is his lament on the death of Richard Cœur de Lion. Of
Uc de la Bacalaria (arrondissement de Scarlat, Dordogne) we have some five or six pieces, including a
well-known *alba*; Jausbert de Puycibot was also from
the Dordogne. Uc de Saint-Circ, the author of various

---

[1] See Strònski, *La Légende amoureuse de Bertran de Born*, p. 43.
[2] See J. Audiau, *Les Troubadours d'Ussel*, p. 12.
[3] On the name Benauges, see A. Jeanroy and Salverda de Grave,
"Poésies de Uc de Saint-Circ", *Bibliothèque Méridionale*, Toulouse, 1913,
XV, p. 192.

biographies and of forty-four poems, lived in Languedoc during the earlier years of the thirteenth century. In view of the large amount of troubadour literature that has perished and of the fact that we are dependent upon allusions in that literature for our knowledge of this side of Savaric's life, we may infer that he was not only a patron of poets, but probably produced poems which have not survived.

So long ago as 1848 Wackernagel pointed to Isidore (*Etym. lib.* 1. 26, De Notis digitorum; Migne, *Patr. Lat.* LXXXII, p. 100) as the origin of the theme of this *tenso*. Isidore may have accepted a misinterpretation of Solomon's Proverbs vi. 13, "Annuit oculis, terit pede, digito loquitur", as referring to a woman's treatment of three lovers. The literature on the subject is summarised in an article by E. Lommatzsch, *Archiv für das Studium der neueren Sprachen*, 1916, CXXXIV, p. 385, who restores to Cn. Naevius the lines from his *Tarentilla*,

> Quasi in choro ludens datatim dat se et communem facit,
> Alii adnutat, alii adnictat, alium amat, alium tenet,
> Alibi manus est occupata, alii percellit pedem,
> Annulum dat alii spectandum, a labris alium invocat,
> Cum aliis cantat, at tamen alii suo dat digito litteras.

In Theocritus I. 36 occurs a similar scene with two lovers.

In close relations with Savaric was the troubadour Uc de Saint-Circ, who began life at Rocamadour, was in Languedoc between 1211 and 1220, visited Spain and ended his life in Italy, whither he probably was driven into exile by the Albigeois wars.[1] "For a long time",

---

[1] A. Jeanroy and Salverda de Grave, "Poésies de Uc de Saint-Circ", *Bibliothèque Méridionale*, Toulouse, 1913, XV, p. xii.

says his biographer, "he was with the countess of Benauges and through her he gained the friendship of Sir
Savaric of Mauléon, who gave him harness and dress."
He relates the circumstances which produced Savaric's
second *tenso* as follows:

I told you of Sir Savaric that he was indeed the root of all
courtesy in the world, and in all good deeds that can be
attributed to man he was the master of all. And he had long
loved and honoured a fair lady of Gascony, my lady
Guilhelma of Benauges, who was the wife of Sir Pierre de
Gavaret,[1] who was viscount of Benauges and lord of S.
Macari and of Lengo;[2] and I can truly say that never did
man do such good deeds for any woman. For a long time
the lady kept him satisfied with her empty promises and
with fair commands and presents, and made him come often
from Poitou to Gascony by land and sea; and when he had
come she was able to deceive him with pretexts so that she
never gave him any pleasure of love. And he was so
enamoured that he did not perceive the deceit, but his
friends opened his eyes and showed him a lady of Armagnac,[3]
the wife of Sir Giraut of Armagnac, young, fair and attractive
and anxious for reputation and to see Sir Savaric for the
good which she had heard of him. And when Sir Savaric
saw the lady, he was much pleased and begged for her love.
And the lady for the great worth that she saw in him, took
him for her knight and named the day when he could come
to her to gain his desire. And he went away very gaily and
returned to Poitou.

In no long time my lady Guilhelma knew the fact, and
how she had appointed a day for him to come to her. Then
she was very jealous and sad because she had not kept him.
She sent a letter and messages and greetings as lovingly as
she could, and told Savaric to come secretly to her at

[1] A troubadour of whose poems only one remains, and that extremely
obscene.   [2] Saint Macaire and Langon in Gironde.
[3] Chabaneau's certain conjecture for de Manchac. The lady was
Mascarosa, the wife of Geraud IV, Count of Armagnac, 1190–1219
(Bergert, *Die von den Trobadors genannten oder gefeierten Damen*, Halle, 1913,
p. 30).

Benauges to have his pleasure of her on the same day that the countess of Armagnac had given him. And know of a truth that I, Uc de S. Circ who have written this explanation, was the messenger that went there and bore all the messages and writings. And in his court was the Provost of Limoges, a man of worth and education and a good troubadour. Savaric, to honour him, explained the whole case and what each lady had said and promised. Savaric said to the Provost that he would ask him of it in a song, and that he proposed a tenso to him, to which of these two should he go on the day that they had given him. And the Provost began and said:[1]

I. Savaric, I ask you to tell me in song your opinion of a worthy knight who has long wooed a lady and she scorns him; then he woos another who becomes his love and gives him a day to meet her and gain his desire. And when the other knows the fact, she sends a message that on the same day she will give him the pleasure which he desired. They are of equal worth and beauty, so choose to which he is to go.

II. Provost, true lovers do not keep changing their hearts but love loyally. Although they may pretend to go and woo another, yet they will never leave the one on whom their affection is set; for a man should by no means change his heart for a deception, but should expect good hope from her who held herself dear. Thither let him make his way, for I do not think that she will deceive him after he has come at her request.

III. Sir, there will be harm done if she, who has him in thrall, has found him attractive and does not keep her promise, in spite of his love and kindness. He will certainly act childishly, if he goes not to her who showed him favour and does not abandon her who tormented him; for she had no intention of rewarding him, nor did it please her to remember his entreaties. But now, when she sees that he could live without her, she dies of jealousy and sends him a message for no other reason than that she does not desire his success elsewhere.

[1] For text see Appendix 8.

IV. Provost, a fickle lady does not give her heart to all and sundry, and they do not understand that she may show sound sense therein. For ladies do not act as one wishes, until they have ascertained that one loves them without deceit. But a woman who is not bound by love, is ready to please everyone and quickly promises her favours; wherefore I fear that if another were to come, she would receive him likewise, and it is better to die of love than to gain one whom all will have.

V. Sir, Ladies destroy love when they postpone their gifts and promises; for he who gives quickly exalts and increases his gifts; for a gift quickly given is worth as much as one postponed, after the time for it has gone by; for a gift cannot be worth so much as it is at the time when one desires to have it, and you then consider as foolishness what one should chiefly welcome; so that a lady is sensible who makes her gift before one has the anxiety (of waiting for it).

VI. Provost, the hard toil and the grievous heavy trouble and torment which I have endured would be pleasure, if my lady would send me a glove and summon me to see her once again before I die; for at her command I would go morning or evening, for with her I wish to abide (even in death) on whose account I know that it (death) would come to me if I had joy through love. But love inflames me and quenches her ardour and I am dying of suffering.

VII. Sir, of that let lady Guilhelma of Benauges be the judge at her pleasure, and I would that Maria of Ventadorn were there and the lady of Monferran, for the three are without deceit.

VIII. Provost, they know so much of love that I accept their decision.

There are two obscure points to which Jeanroy has called attention,[1] in this affair. Why should the Provost propose the question? Savaric was the one who needed advice, he surely should have asked for it. And why

---

[1] *Annales du Midi*, II, p. 442.

should the Provost propose as judge the lady against whom he has been arguing? Possibly the account given in the *razo* is incomplete or apocryphal.

Uc de Saint-Circ's relations with Savaric seem to fall between the years 1211 and 1219, in which year Savaric went crusading. Of the three ladies mentioned, Guilhelma is named in documents dated 1219 and 1228 (Chabaneau); Maria of Ventadorn was alive in 1221 (Strònski, p. 61) and the Viscountess of Montferrand, the wife of the Dauphin Robert of Auvergne, made a will in 1219 (Jeanroy and Salverda de Grave, p. 153). Uc refers to Gardacors, Savaric's *senhal* for Guilhelma (J. and S. de G. no. 1, l. 61)

> Seign'En Savaric, mout plaing
> Gardacors, car per estaing
> Camjet son aur fin valen
> E·l clar maragde luzen
> Per veir'escur que luzir
> Non pot mais ni resplandir.

Sir Savaric, I am sorry for Gardacors that she has changed her fine precious gold for tin, and her bright and shining emerald for tarnished glass which cannot gleam nor shine.

This appears to allude to the lady as fickle. In no. XIII, he praises her as a paragon of worth, if this poem is his and not Savaric's. Two other poems are dedicated to Savaric, one being sent to Esnendes in the neighbourhood of La Rochelle. Savaric became Seneschal of Gascony in 1205, and the helper of Raimon of Toulouse in the Albigeois war in 1211; it is not possible to say which of these events brought him in contact with Uc de Saint-Circ.

Savaric enjoyed a considerable reputation both during his lifetime and posthumously. He is mentioned in the *Roman de la Rose* (or *de Guillaume de Dole*) by Jean Renart, a poem composed between 1212 and 1213, as may be inferred from numerous references to historical characters. Savaric appears in a catalogue of distinguished visitors who arrive for a tournament:

> Et cil Gauchiers de Chastillion
> Et uns autres de Mauleon.   (ll. 2097–8)

Francesco Redi regarded him as an Englishman: "Salvarico di Malleone, inglese, poeta provenzale" (*Bacco in Toscana*, p. 100). So also did Jean de Nostre-dame: "Savaric de Mauléon fut gentilhomme, anglais de nation."[1] *Guillaume de la Barre* is a somewhat monotonous *roman d'aventure*, composed by Arnaud Vidal of Castelnaudary in 1318. Guillaume is sent to fetch the daughter of the King of England as a wife for his master, the King of La Serra; after a voyage of thirty days they arrive:

> En.i. port d'un noble baro,
> Senhors era de Malleo,
> Hont Hom paguava trautage
> .C. bezans d'aur hom de parage
> Solamens, si fos cavaliers,
> E.xxx. si fos escudiers,
> E bezan bezan per garsso.   (ll. 123–9)

in the harbour of a noble baron; he was lord of Mauléon to whom toll was paid, 100 besants for a man of noble birth only, 30 if he were a squire and one for each of the rank and file.

---

[1] *Les vies des plus célèbres poètes provensaux*, ed. Chabaneau-Anglade, p. 66; Rita Lejeune Dehousse, "L'Œuvre de Jean Renart", *Bibliothèque de la Faculté de Philosophie et Lettres de l'Université de Liège*, fasc. LXI, p. 100. Audiau, *Les Troubadours et l'Angleterre*, p. 25.

The lord's castle is repeatedly mentioned:

> El castels fo d'obra talhada,
> Espes de torrs e ben dechatz
> Malleos, e fo be guardtz. (ll. 154–6)

The castle was of cut stone, thick, with towers and was well called Mauléon and was well guarded.

It is possible that dim traditions or reminiscences of Savaric and La Rochelle may have suggested the description and choice of name. The poet certainly makes the Lord of Malleo a Saracen, but this is necessary for the development of his tale. The editor (P. Meyer, *Anc. Textes français*, 1895, p. xliv) points out that the names of the heroes, Chabert and Guillaume de le Barre, "sont les noms du Midi"; but he has made no observations upon Malleo.

Contemporary writers have passed no judgment upon the character of Savaric, with the exception of the author of the Provençal life whose testimony cannot be regarded as authoritative; judgment upon such figures in the twelfth or thirteenth centuries can be formed only by a consideration of their acts, a consideration unbiased by the political or moral standards of our own times. In comparison with such members of the Poitevin nobility as the ambitious and resentful Lusignans, Savaric stands out as an attractive character. He was as loyal to John and to Henry III as they deserved, and did not abandon their causes until their desertion of him showed that he had no other means of saving his own; if Henry had given him any reasonable support, he would have been able to keep La Rochelle. He was energetic, adventurous and prepared to take risks; he refused to be starved to death in Corfe castle, a fate which befell others of John's prisoners. Nor was he unwilling to speak his mind to those in authority, as he spoke to John at the siege of Rochester. A good soldier of the fighting type, with some notions of strategy, his failures were due to the composite character of the forces under his command or to the incompetence of leaders with whom he was associated. He regarded war as a means of profit, as did the majority of his contemporaries, who were attracted to a battle or a tournament by hopes of loot and ransom; his extortion of money from Raimon of Toulouse is difficult to excuse, but he was far above the level of ruffians like Martin Algais or Walter Buck, and his action at Croyland showed a respect for the Church and a dislike for senseless destruction which may have been repeated on other occasions. It is remarkable that Savaric was able to retain the confidence of such a man as John, whom Petit-Dutaillis[1] considers to have been a maniac, suffering from a disease now known to alienists as periodic psychosis or cyclothumia; Savaric was perhaps one of those vigorous and domineering characters who can impose themselves upon the weak-minded and oblige them to follow and obey, when their malady attacks them. He was a competent administrator, and his record in Poitou was a creditable achievement, in view of the difficulties which beset his steps. Whether his considerable generosity to religious foundations and his crusading venture were actuated by genuine religious feeling or were in the nature of insurance against the terrors of the next world, it is impos-

---

[1] *La Monarchie Féodale en France et en Angleterre*, Paris, 1933, pp. 240 ff. His diagnosis from the facts of John's career is interesting, and to the non-medical mind, plausible.

sible to say. It is a matter for regret that Savaric, whose
life is better known to us than that of any other troubadour, should have left so little poetry behind him; but it
is noticeable that the troubadours whose surviving
poems are most numerous are generally those of whose
lives little is known. An aristocrat, as Savaric was,
depended in no way upon his art for a livelihood, and
regarding it rather as an amusement than as a business,
may not have produced much and was under no
necessity of pushing himself and his productions into the
notice of patrons. In short, Savaric appears as an out-
standing figure among the aristocracy of his age, and
his considerable reputation was not due merely to the
accident of noble birth, but primarily to native talent
and to force of character.

III
APPENDICES
*

1. The Family of Mauléon

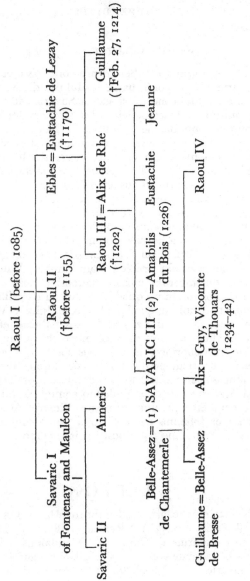

Raoul I (before 1085)

Savaric I of Fontenay and Mauléon | Raoul II (†before 1155) | Ebles=Eustachie de Lezay (†1170)

Aimeric | Raoul III=Alix de Rhé (†1202) | Guillaume (†Feb. 27, 1214)

Savaric II | Belle-Assez=(1) SAVARIC III (2)=Amabilis du Bois (1226) | Eustachie | Jeanne

de Chantemerle

Guillaume=Belle-Assez | Alix=Guy, Vicomte de Thouars (1234–42) | Raoul IV

de Bresse

6-2

2. Rotula Chartorum (p. 24).

Johannes Dei gratia etc. Sciatis nos concessisse et hac presenti carta nostra confirmasse Radulpho de Malleone et Willelmo de Malleone fratri suo et Savarico filio ejusdem Radulphi totum Talemondeis et les Mostiers des Mafeiz et Curson cum omnibus pertinentibus de Talemendiis [*sic*] in homagio [et serviciis *erased*] et dominicis et redditionibus pro jure suo quod ipsi et antecessores sui habuerunt et tenuerunt in Rupella. Et predicta concessimus eisdem et carta nostra confirmavimus et heredibus eorum decem milia solidorum monete Pictavie annuatim sibi percipiendorum in preposita terra de Rupella. Et post ea predicta castrum de Banaum cum omnibus pertinentibus suis ejusdem castri, excepta porcione quam Hugo de Tuarz tenuit die qua ista carta facta fuit. Et pro hac concessione et confirmacione nostra predicti Radulphus et Willelmus et Savaricus quietaverunt nobis et heredibus nostris de se et heredibus suis totum jus quod habebant in Rupella. Quare volumus et precipimus quod predicti Radulphus et Willelmus et Savaricus et heredes sui post ipsos habeant et teneant omnia predicta bene et in pace, libere et quiete, integre, plenarie et honorifice, in omnibus locis et rebus ad ea pertinentibus, sicut predictum est, sic rationabilis carta et carta matris nostre, quas inde habent, testantur. Teste Rege, Sancti Andreae episcopo, Willelmo comite Arundel, Hugo de Gornaco etc. Datum per manus Simonis Archidiaconi Wellensis et Johannis de Grai apud Cenomannum, XXX die Septembris, anno regni nostri primo (1199).

3. La Tor Corp.

This is certainly the form used in the royal letter of August 20, 1203 (Rot. Pat. 1, p. 33 b): "Rex etc. Willelmo de Blundville etc. constabularius de Corp etc. Mandamus vobis quod accepta bona gente vobiscum sine dilacione adducatis nobis salvo Savaricum de Maloleone et Americum de Forç usque in Normanniam dimissa tali gente in castro nostro de Corp, quo illud melius custodiatur quam custoditum fuit quando predictus Savaricus cepit et tenuit contra nos turrim, et super omnia videatis quod salvo nobis adducantur predicti Savaricus et Americus et in hujus rei etc. Teste me ipso apud Vernolium xx die Augusti." Corp is written with an abbreviated *p*; later entries refer to W. de Blundville as the constable of Corf or Corfe and there is no doubt that Corp in this letter is a scribe's error. Why the same form should appear in the Provençal *razo* is difficult to explain; it is hardly likely that the author of it had seen or heard of this letter.

John appears to have been on good terms with Savaric's uncle; on March 15, 1202, he issued an order "ballivis Normanniae salutem; mandamus vobis quod unam navatam avene quam dilectus et fidelis noster Willelmus de Maloleone habet carcatam permittatis sine impedimento ire in Pictaviam."[1] On November 2, William has the option of being included in a truce between the king and the Viscount of Thouars.[2] No doubt John's knowledge of the family predisposed him to bring Savaric over to his service.

4. Rot. Pat. 1, p. 55 b. Obsides Savarici de Maloleone.

Mater ipsius Savarici
Uxor ipsius Savarici
Filia Emerici de Forz
Filius Brieni de Monte Acuto
} sunt apud Northanton.

Willelmus Johannis cum Justiciario
Willelmus Thaharry cum Simone de Kima
Simonus Auberti cum Girardo de Canvilla
Theobaldus Jakesin cum Comite Alberico
Petrus Meynardy cum domino Cantuarie
Willelmus de Vilates cum Comite de Ferrariis
Aimericus de Chaucy cum Roberto de Marmiune

[1] Rot. Pat. 1, p. 7.   [2] *Ibid.* p. 21.

Filius Chalonis de Metulo ⎫
Filius Willelmi de Viteri ⎬ cum domino Cantuarie
Filius H. Auri cum Comite Rogero
Hugo de Almania cum Warino filio Gerardi
Filius Hugonis de Nuille cum Rege
Filius Rannulfi de Nassun cum Episcopo Cicestrensi.

Orders for the return of the first three to La Rochelle were issued on June 19 and June 27, 1206 (Rot. Pat. 1, pp. 67 b, 66 b).

5. Rot. Pat. p. 67 b.

Rex omnibus etc. de Engolisme et de comite Engolisme etc. Mandamus vobis quod sacramentum fidelitatis domine vestre Regine uxoris nostre coram dilecto et fideli seniori nostro Savarico de Maloleone quod fidem ei tenebitis tanquam domine ligie vestre contra omnes mortales salva fide nostra quamdiu vixerimus et ita quod nec civitatem nec castrum nec fortaleciam alii quam illi vel precepto suo liberabitis cum de nobis humanitas contigerit. Teste me ipso apud Rupellam quarto die Novembris anno etc. viii (1206).

6. King John's Will.

Ego J. Dei gratia, Rex Anglie, dominus Hibernie, dux Norm' et Aquit' comes Andegav' gravi infirmitate preventus, nec sufficiens ad tempus infirmitatis mee currere per singula, ut testamentum meum de singulis rebus meis condam; ordinationem et dispositionem testamenti mei fidei et dispositioni legitime committo fidelium meorum subscriptorum, sine quorum consilio, etiam in bono statu constitutus, nullatenus in presentia eorum testamentum meum ordinarem; ut quod ipsi fideliter ordinaverint et disposuerint de rebus meis, tam in satisfactione facienda Deo et sancte ecclesie de dampnis et injuriis eis illatis, quam in succursu faciendo terre Jerosolimitane, et sustentatione prestanda filiis meis pro hereditate sua perquirenda et defendenda, et in remuneratione facienda illis qui fideliter nobis servierunt, et in distributione facienda pauperibus et domibus religiosis pro salute anime mee, ratum sit et firmum. Peto etiam, ut qui consilium et juvamen eis fecerit ad testamentum meum ordinandum, gratiam Dei percipiat et favorem: qui autem ordinationem et dispositionem suam infregerit, maledictionem et indignationem Omnipotentis Dei et beate Marie et omnium sanctorum incurrat. Imprimis igitur volo, quod corpus meum sepeliatur in ecclesia sancte Marie et sancti Wulstani de Wigorn'. Ordinatores autem et dispositores tales constituo. Dominum G. Dei gratia, tit' sancti Martini presbiterum cardinalem, apostolice sedis legatum.

> Dominum P. Winton' episcopum.
> Dominum R. Cicestren' episcopum.
> Dominum S. Wigorn' episcopum.
> Fratrem Aimericum de sancta Maura.
> W. Marescallum comitem Penbroc'.
> R. com' Cestr'.
> Willielmum comitem de Ferrariis.
> Willielmum Bruwne.
> Walterum de Lascy, etc.
> Johannem de Monemunt.
> Savaricum de Malo Leone.
> Falkesium de Breaute.[1]

7. E. Lommatzsch, *Provenzalisches Liederbuch*, Berlin, 1917, p. 192.

Savaric de Mauléon

> Gaucelm, tres jocs enamoratz
> Partisc a vos et a n'Ugo,
> E chascus prendetz lo plus bo
> E laissatz me qualque·us volhatz:
> Una domn'a tres preiadors,
> E destre nhla tan lor amors

[1] Rymer, *Foedera*, I, p. 144.

Que, quan tuit trei li son denan,
A chascun fai d'amor semblan:
L'un esgard' amorozamen,
L'autr' estrenh la man doussamen,
Al tertz caussiga·l pe rizen.
Digatz, al qual, pos aissi es,
Fai major amor de totz tres?

Gaucelm Faidit

Senh' en Savaric, ben sapchatz
Que l'amics recep plus gen do
Qu'es francamen, ses cor felo,
Dels bels olhs plazens esgardatz.
Del cor mou aquela doussors,
Per qu'es cen tans maier honors.
E del man tener dic aitan,
Que non li ten ni pro ni dan,
Qu'aital plazer comunalmen
Fan domnas per acolhimen.
E del caussigar non enten
Que la domn' amor li fezes,
Ni deu per amor esser pres.

Uc de la Bacalaria

Gaucelm, vos dizetz so que·us platz,
For que non mantenetz razo,
Qu'en l'esgardar non conosc pro
A l'amic, que vos razonatz;
E s'el i enten, es folers,
Qu'olh esgardan lui et alhors
E nulh autre poder non an.
Mas quan la blanca mas ses gan
Estrenh son amic doussamen,
L'amors mou del cor e del sen.
E'n Savarics, car part tan gen,
Mantenga·l caussigar cortes
De pe, qu'eu no·l mantenrai ges.

Savaric de Mauléon

Senher, pos lo melhs mi laissatz,
Mantenrai·l eu, ses dir de no;
Don dic que·l caussigars que fo
Faitz del pe fo fin' amistatz,
Celada de lauzenjadors,
E par be, pos aital socors
Pres l'amics rizen caussigan,
Que l'amors es ses tot enjan.
E qui·l tener de la man pren
Per major amor, fai nonsen.
E d'en Gaucelm no m'es parven
Que l'esgart per melhor prezes,
Si tan com ditz d'amor saubes.

Gaucelm Faidit

Senher, vos que l'esgart blasmatz
Dels olhs e lor plazen faisso,
No sabetz que messatgier so
Del cor que·ls i a enviatz;
Qu'olh descobron als amadors
So que reten el cor paors,
Don totz los plazers d'amor fan.
E maintas vetz rizen gaban
Caussiga·l pe a mainta gen
Domna ses autr' entendemen.
E n'Ugo mante falhimen,
Que·l teners de man non es res,
Ni non cre qu'anc d'amor mogues.

Uc de la Bacalaria

Gaucelm, encontr' amor parlatz,
Vos e·l senher de Malleo,
E pareis ben a la tenso
Que·ls olhs que vos avetz triatz
E que razonatz pels melhors
An trahitz mains entendedors.

E de la domn' ab cor truan,
Si·m cassigava·l pe un an,
Non auria mon cor jauzen.
E de la man es ses conten
Que l'estrenhers val per un cen,
Car ja, si al cor non plagues,
L'amors no l'agr' al man trames.

Savaric de Mauléon

Gaucelm, vencutz es el conten
Vos e n'Ugo, certanamen,
E volh que·n fassa·l jutjamen
Mos Gardacors que m'a conques,
E na Mari', on bos pretz es.

Gaucelm Faidit

Senher, vencutz no sui nien,
Et al jutgar er ben parven,
Per qu'eu volh que·i si' eissamen
Na Guilhelma de Benauges
Ab sos ditz amoros cortes.

Uc de la Bacalaria

Gaucelm, tant ai razo valen
Qu'amdos vos fortz e mi defen;
E sai un' ab gai cors plazen
En que·l jutjamens fora mes,
Mas pro, vei, n'i a mais de tres.

8. A. Kolsen, *Dichtungen der Trobadors*, Halle, 1916, p. 14.

I

I   Savaric, e·us deman
Qe·m digatz en chantan
D'un cavallier valen,
Q'a preiat longamen
Una dompna prezan,
Et ill met l'en soan,

Puois prega n'autra, q'esdeven s'amia
   E dona·il jorn c'ab lieis sia
   Per penre tot son voler;
   E qand l'autra·n sap lo ver,
   Manda·il q'aqel mezeis dia
   Li dara·l joi, qe·il qeria.
   D'engal pretz e d'un semblan
   Son, e chauzetz a cal an.

II

   Prebost, li fin aman
   Non van lor cor camjan,
   Anz amon leialmen;
   Si tot si fant parven
   C'anon aillors preian,
   Ges per tant no·s partran
De lai on an assis lor drudaria,
   Car ges per una fadia
   No·n deu hom son cor mover,
   Anz atenda·l bon esper
   De lieis q'en car se tenia.
   Lai se prend'e teingna via,
   Qu'eu non pens q'ella l'engan,
   Pois er vengutz a son man.

III

   Seigner, et aura·i dan,
   S'ella, q'a son coman,
   L'a trobat avinen
   Ni n'intra son coven
   Per so car l'am'e blan!
   Ben aura sen d'enfan,
S'a lieis non vai, q'en grat lo retenia,
   E lais lieis que l'aucizia;
   C'anc jorn no·l volc pro tener
   Ni·l plac sos precs retener.
   Mas ar qand ve que viuria
   Sens lieis, mor de gelosia
   E per als no·il vai mandan
   Mas car no·n vol que ben l'an.

IV

Dompn'ab leugier talan
Non ama tan ni qan,
Prebost, ni non enten
Que puosc' aver gran sen.
Car ges dompnas non fan
So c'om vol, tro que an
Conogut c'om las ama ses bausia;
   Mas cella, c'amors non lia,
   Vol a totz faire plazer
   E promet tost lo jazer,
   Per qe·m pes, s'autre venia,
   C'atressi lo·s colgaria,
   Et es mieills c'om moir' aman
   C'aia lieis, don tuich l'auran.

V

Seigner, amor desfan
Dompnas, que vant loignan
Lor don e prometen;
Car qui dona breumen,
Fai son don aut e gran;
Q'us dos val atretan
C'om dona tost cum cel c'om loignaria,
   Pois la sazos passaria.
   Car dos non pot tant valer
   Cum qand hom lo vol aver,
   E vos tenetz a foillia
   So c'om plus grazir deuria;
   Que sen fai, qand don'avan
   Dompna c'om n'auja·l masan.

VI

Prebost, li dur afan
E·il greu maltraich pesan,
C'ai sofert, e·il tormen
Mi serion plazen,
Si·m trameti'un gan
Ma dompn'e·m mandes tan

C'una vetz, anz que moris, la veiria;
   Q'a son mandamen iria
   O de maitin o de ser,
   Per c'ab leis vuoil remaner
   Per cui sai que m'avenria,
   Si joi per amor avia.
   Mas mi art e lieis escan
   Amors e muor sofertan.

VII

Seigner, d'aisso jutge·l ver
Na Guillelm'a son plazer
De Benaug'e na Maria
De Ventadorn vuoill qu'i sia
E·il dompna de Mon ferran;
Qe las tres son ses engan.

VIII

Prebost, d'amor sabon tan
Qu'eu n'autrei so qu'en diran.

INDEX

Albigenses, 19–24, 49
Alix de Ré, 4, 14
Amabilis du Bois, 59
Angoulême, 43
Arthur, 10, 12, 13

Bedford, 32, 49
Belle-Assez, 5, 14
Berengère, 50
Bernard de Ventadorn, 65
Bertran de Born, 4, 13, 16
Bigod, Roger, 33
Blanche of Castile, 11, 50, 56, 57
Bordeaux, 25, 42, 47, 52
Bouvines, 25, 27
Boves, Hugh of, 29
Brabant, 21, 30, 31
Bréauté, Falkes de, 30, 32, 49, 51
Brienne, Jean de, 39
Bristol, 35, 37
Buck, Walter, 30, 32, 33
Burgh, Hubert de, 16, 26, 45, 52, 54
Bury, 33

Castelnaudary, 21–23
Cercamon, 65
Châtelaillon, 5, 24
Coggeshall, 33
Colchester, 33
Corfe, 13, 14, 35
Cornwall, Richard of, 54, 55, 56
Croyland, 35, 36

Damietta, 40, 44
Damme, 24, 26
Dover, 29
Dublin, 28

Ebles de Mauléon, 3, 9
Eleanor of Aquitaine, 7, 8, 9, 24, 65
Eleanor of Aragon, 20, 21
Ely, 33

Eustachie de Chatellerault, 4
Eustachie de Lezay, 4

Fécamp, 24
Ferrand, 24, 25
Foulques de Mauléon, 3

Gaucelm Faidit, 68, 70
Gautier, Hubert, 14
Gloucester, 36
Genoa, 39, 41
Geoffrey of Brittany, 65
Geoffrey of Lusignan, 12, 26, 57
Gualo, 36, 37
Guilhelma de Benauges, 70, 72
Guillaume de Mauléon, 4, 15, 18
Guillaume des Roches, 15, 18, 26

Henry II, 4, 9, 20, 31, 65
Henry III, 32, 36, 41 ff.
Honorius III, 33, 37, 39, 51, 55, 60
Hugh Le Brun, 11, 12, 26

Ingeburge, 10
Innocent III, 11, 43, 44, 45, 48
Isabel of Angoulême, 11, 43, 44, 45, 48
Isemburge, 50

Jausbert de Puycibot, 65, 66
Jeanne de Rochechouart, 4
Joan, 26, 43
John Lackland, 5, 10, 25–26, 65
John, King of Jerusalem, 50
Joppa, 4

King's Lynn, 36

La Rochelle, 4, 9, 16, 18, 25, 42, 46–48, 50–55
Le Mans, 12
Lincoln, 35
London, 34, 46

Louis VIII of France, 11, 24, 34, 48
Louis IX, 56
Lusignan, house of, 11, 26, 43–45, 47–49, 50

Map, Walter, 31
Marcabru, 65
Maria of Ventadorn, 70
Marshal, William the, 26, 36, 37
Mauclerc, Peter, 55, 56, 57
Mirebeau, 12

Neville, Geoffrey de, 43, 49
Newark, 36
Niort, 15, 42, 43, 47, 50

Otho of Saxony, 7, 24, 25, 65

Pandulf, 45, 46
Parthenay-Larchévêque, 3, 45
Peire Bremon Ricas Novas, 58
Philippe Auguste, 7, 8, 10, 24, 42, 48
Portsmouth, 48

Raimon VI, 19
Raimon VII, 20, 55
Raoul de Mauléon, I, II, III, 3, 4; IV, 59
Reading, 28

Richard Cœur de Lion, 4, 7, 65
Ré, 25, 53
Rochester, 29
Routiers, 31
Rudel, 55, 56, 67

Salisbury, Earl of, 25, 30, 53, 54
Saracens, 4
Savaric I and II, 3
Savaric III, 4, 5, 10, 15, 16, 18, 21–23
Simon de Montfort, 20, 22, 23, 25, 27
Soissons, Council of, 24
Sordello, 58
Spalding, 35
Staines, 27

Talmond, 4, 10, 38
Thouars, 3, 16, 18, 47, 50
Thouars, Hugh de, 18
Tilty, 32
Toulouse, 20
Turnham, Robert de, 15, 16

Uc de la Bacalaria, 68, 70, 71
Uc de Saint-Circ, 67

William IX of Poitiers, 65
Winchester, 28, 29, 34
Worcester, 36

Printed in the United States
By Bookmasters